Shared Reading

Frank McTeague

Shared Reading

in the middle and high school years

HEINEMANN
Portsmouth, NH

© 1992 Pembroke Publishers Limited
Pembroke Publishers Limited
528 Hood Road
Markham, Ontario
L3R 3K9

Published in the U.S.A. by
Heinemann Educational Books, Inc.
361 Hanover Street,
Portsmouth, N.H. 03801-3959
ISBN (U.S.) 0-435-08735-5

Canadian Cataloguing in Publication Data

McTeague, Frank
  Shared reading in the middle and high school
years

Includes bibliographical references.
ISBN 0-921217-78-1

1. Reading (Secondary). 2. High school students –
Books and reading. 3. Literature – Study and
teaching (Secondary). I. Title.

LB1632.M37 1992   428.4'0712   C92-093085-9

Acknowledgments
page 6: From "Textuality: Power and Pleasure" in *English Education*, May 1987. Copyright 1987 by the National Council of Teachers of English. Reprinted with permission.

page 46: Excerpt from *On Teaching Literature* by Northrop Frye, copyright © 1972 by Harcourt Brace Jovanovich, Inc., reprinted by permission of the publisher.

page 65: Reprinted with permission of Thimble Press, Station Road, Woodchester, Stroud, Glos, U.K. GL5 5EQ.

Editor: Elynor Kagan
Design: John Zehethofer
Cover Illustration: Graham Pilsworth
Typesetting: Jay Tee Graphics Ltd

Printed and bound in Canada
9 8 7 6 5 4 3 2 1

For their spirit of collaboration and for their valuable contribu-
tions, I am most grateful to my colleagues, the English teachers
in the city of York schools, especially Heather Bichan, Mark
Brubacher, Bonnie Foord, Doug Hilker, Gary Hophan, Ryder
Payne, Helen Porter and Brenda Protheroe.

For his inspiration and support throughout the entire process,
I am deeply indebted to Jerry George, Education Officer with
the Ontario Ministry of Education.

In my view the literature classroom should be the most exciting and productive in the whole school — not because it is a shrine for great works but because it is the place where students experience their own productive possibilities, the place of entry, for them, into the cultural web of textuality: the place where they can see the textual apparatus from the inside and learn how to pull the strings themselves. To make this possibility a reality in our classrooms we must begin by doing one big simple thing. We must accept as the center of our enterprise the study of all the forms of sign and symbol that seek power over us or offer us pleasure.

Robert Scholes

Contents

Foreword

The intention of this book is to focus on the contextual realities of every class in which literature is taught. Each class has an assortment of individuals who have a range of characteristics emerging from the diversity of their personal backgrounds:

- their ethnic, cultural and linguistic roots;
- their personal maturity — cognitive, affective and ethical;
- their previous experience, which has shaped personal beliefs and attitudes about themselves and about school, books and literature;
- their present circumstances and expectations.

All of these are factors that teachers must consider carefully in selecting the literary works to be presented and in making decisions about the literary goals to be pursued and how best to pursue them. These factors will determine, to a considerable extent, the quality of the reading, the discussion and the general apprehension of the literary experiences provided. Indeed, it is now an established and widely accepted principle that the act of reading is a socio-psycholinguistic process in which readers reconstruct meaning from texts. The success or the quality of the reading process is determined by two main sources of meaning: what readers bring to the text and what the text brings to the reader. This is true for any reading situation, from functional to aesthetic.

It is also true that reading (like listening) is a receptive mode of language use (as speaking and writing are expressive modes). As a receptive mode reading is primarily private, personal and individualistic. But in a classroom the private and personal experience can be extended, enriched and diversified by the group, if the teacher can transform the class from a collection of private readers (each at a different level of development) to a community that includes not only readers, but also writers and talkers. The difference — and it is a critical difference — between private personal reading and the shared reading by a class lies in co-operative learning. For literature classes this collaborative process allows students to explore, probe and discover texts, and come to value a more illumined and engaged response to any literary experience.

In guiding the class from private to shared response, the teacher plays a critical role by creating a context in which the individuals "share their secrets" (Meek, 1982). This book presents teachers with specific strategies to help them in this process. The methods suggested here are garnered from the research and development of such leaders as Aidan Chambers, Jack Thompson, John Dixon, Nancie Atwell, James Moffett, David Booth and Bob Barton.

This book invites teachers to try out these strategies, to take ownership of them, to become comfortable and competent with them. It is hoped that these strategies will empower teachers to draw their students into a new relationship with literature, a new relationship with each other, and a new relationship with their teachers.

1. Exploring the Realms of Response

What Is Response to Literature?

Response to Literature is a classroom strategy in which teachers arrange for students to explore a text in small groups and to share their personal insights with each other. Teachers who are familiar with the research and curriculum developments associated with the general field of "response theory" have found that it has enabled them:

- to re-define literature and their teaching of it;
- to select better literary works and hence a wider range of literary experiences;
- to have students read more widely and deeply in the literary field;
- to increase students' enjoyment of their reading experience as their insights and sensitivity to text deepen;
- to broaden and diversify classroom activities that support the processes of inquiry, probing, exploring and extending the meaning of the text;
- to reconceptualize teaching, learning and evaluation in the English program.

Teachers who make the departure from the traditional analytical approach, with its naming of parts, comprehension questions and other paraphernalia, find new excitement and satisfaction in their classrooms. The albatross of teaching literary criticism has been lifted from their shoulders. The teacher's voice no longer dominates the classroom. The questions raised by students become the new agenda; the suggestions made by students guide the follow-up activity; the insights engendered by students direct the focus or thrust of the inquiry. These teachers discover, as Margaret Meek (1982) observed, "Children offer us the evidence we need but we so rarely see it for what it is."

Close reading and wide reading should not be thought of as quite separate activities. Active response to a work of literature involves what might be called an unspoken monologue of responses — a fabric of comment, speculation, relevant autobiography. . . . Talk in class should arise from and further stimulate the individual monologues of response.

James Britton

What Is Response to Literature Teaching?

A literary work comes into being afresh when it is read by someone who is willing to undertake an open-minded transaction with the text. The reader gives her attention to the text, lets the text speak to her in all the literary qualities she can perceive. The response to literature approach proposes that the individual experience of the text, different for each reader, should be our main focus in the classroom treatment of literature. The teacher's reading of the text, although it is likely an expert interpretation, is only one of many possible readings. Even among expert readers and critics, texts will differ in their interpretation and nuance.

The aim of response to literature teaching is to enable the student to become a better reader, a more discerning responder to the textual experience. Only by becoming a better reader can the student attain the rich and rewarding enjoyment of literature that is the goal of our teaching.

Response to literature teaching inevitably fuses reading, talking and writing in an integrated and interactive process. By talking and writing in response to the reading of literature, the students become more fully engaged in the underlying processes of composing and comprehending. They create their own texts spontaneously to comprehend the given text more fully. These new texts will, of course, be both oral and written.

Central to this process is the negotiation of an author's meaning and intention in small groups. Such interaction is the daily

The following excerpt is taken from an interview by Rhonda Bunbury (1986) with Russell Hoban, the British novelist and author of children's books.

Bunbury: There are students, literary critics, and people interested in reader reception, who would all say that their own responses as readers are as important as the original work of fiction that they're responding to.

Hoban: Absolutely, and I'm the first to assert that the writer is not the final authority on what is written. It's as though you've got somebody up on the masthead: "Land-ho" he says, "we're away . . . three points off the starboard bow." I say, "What is it?" He says "I don't know . . . it's an island, I can see trees." Well he doesn't necessarily know what's on the island, he doesn't know whether there are fresh water springs, he doesn't know whether there are poisonous snakes or flowers or coconuts. When he gets closer he can say that he sees coconut palms or he sees flowers or certain kinds of trees, so he's the one who has first seen the thing and pointed it out, but he is not the final authority on what's there. A geologist following after him or a botanist or biologist would find a lot of things he didn't know about. If you want to make the metaphor a little bit more pointed, the navigator of the ship that found the island doesn't necessarily know what's on the island. Well, when I write a story, I'll see something, I'll find something, and I take it in a certain way, and it has a certain part in my story. There may be all kinds of things there that I haven't thought about and there may be connections between elements in my story that I'm ignorant of, but I always trust in my intuition, that I'm somehow taking in the things that want to be together as elements of a story. The other people can find connections that I couldn't make for myself.

Bunbury: How then should teachers set about teaching literature? Can they teach literature? I know you're the writer so perhaps it's unfair to ask you but you might have a point of view.

Hoban: From time to time I've done writing workshops, and I have found that university students who had studied "English Literature" seemed very often to be handicapped in their writing because they were burdened with ideas about interpretation and analysis. Because they were overwhelmed by a need for structure they felt that there had to be a beginning, a middle, and an end, and they were not able, naturally, to take hold of the thing, wherever it offered a grip. So a natural story-making process — what I think of as a natural mythopoeic process —

> had been interfered with. It was no longer a natural capability. The natural resource had been atrophied, and a laid-on, imposed thing had taken its place.

fare of the English classroom that nurtures both the hearts and minds of our students. By sharing insights, swapping opinions and negotiating meaning in small group situations, students stretch the language they *have* into the new forms of expression they *need* to convey their discoveries.

The teacher circulates from group to group to monitor the progress students are making and to prompt them to penetrate the text — to move beyond the obvious or the superficial. If students happen to be snagged on some minor point or distracted from the text, a few suggestions or questions can steer them toward a more productive inquiry. Such suggestions can be made only after listening with empathy. The more experience students have in this collaborative process, the less the teacher need intervene.

What Is Response to Literature Learning?

When teachers interview students, they often find that many think of themselves as good readers because they read a lot or because they can read fast. Others — a much smaller group — will consider themselves to be poor readers because they don't like reading, their vocabulary is poor or they are having problems trying to concentrate. Indeed, there are many more differences among students. Every classroom teacher faces a group of students at the same grade level who manifest an amazing range of cognitive ability, language competence, creativity and emotional maturity. Moreover, there is a range of attitudes towards books and a range of interests and tastes. Nevertheless, teachers want to reach all students, wherever they may be in these divergent ranges. But knowing or assessing where they are is a quite complex matter. In addition, teachers want to know that the literature program they are providing is making a difference to all their students. Teachers need to be assured that their students are making some progress and that there are signs of improvement. But what are the significant signs of maturity, growth or development in the complex matter of response to literature?

What are the indications of a deepening response, insight and general sophistication in reading strategies?

With such questions in mind Jack Thomson (1986) designed a model or framework to assist teachers by providing some sign-posts to observe and assess students in the various stages of development (see page 16).

The purpose of presenting Professor Thomson's model here is to provide teachers with helpful concepts and key terms. Teachers who are committed to learning more about reader response stages and strategies are urged to read his deserving study, *Understanding Teenagers' Reading*.

Three Classroom Strategies

Three effective classroom strategies growing in popularity are:

- use of reading response journals;
- use of listening logs; and
- guiding students' booktalk.

The Reading Response Journal

The reading response journal is a notebook (or writing folder) in which students record a measure of their enjoyment of a book they have chosen for silent reading under your guidance. Upon completion of a unit, or whole book, the students enter into their reading journals their own personal responses to the reading experience. During the initial trial period, the teacher provides whatever directions, instructions and guidelines that are appropriate for a particular class or group or for individuals within the class. Teachers decide during this initial period whether to arrange writing partners or small groups to share, prepare or support the written response students choose to make. Les Parsons has described this strategy extensively in his book *Response Journals* (1990).

The Listening Log

The listening log is used as a response to the teacher's daily reading aloud from a literary work not otherwise available to the students. There are as many variations of listening logs as there are of reading response journals. By using the procedure below teachers will readily make their own adaptations of the basic

Response to Literature: A Developmental Model (Thomson, 1986)

Process Stages: Kinds of Satisfaction (Requirements for satisfaction at all stages: enjoyment and elementary understanding)	Degree of Intensity of Interest		Degree of Sophistication of Response		Process Strategies
	Weak Passive	Strong Active	Simple and Rudimentary	Developed and Subtle	
1. Unreflective interest in action	↕	↕	↕	↕	(a) Rudimentary mental images (stereotypes from film and television) (b) Predicting what might happen next in the short term
2. Emphathising	↕	↕	↕	↕	(c) Mental images of affect (d) Expectations about characters
3. Analogising	↕	↕	↕	↕	(e) Drawing on the repertoire of personal experiences, making connections between characters and one's own life
4. Reflecting on the significance of events (theme) and behaviour (distanced evaluation of characters)		↕		↕	(f) Generating expectations about alternative possible long-term outcomes (g) Interrogating the text, filling in gaps (h) Formulating puzzles, enigmas, accepting hermeneutic challenges
5. Reviewing the whole work as the author's creation	↕	↕		↕	(i) Drawing on literary and cultural repertoires (j) Interrogating the text to match the author's representation with one's own (k) Recognition of implied author
6. Consciously considered relationship with the author, recognition of textual ideology, and understanding of self (identity theme) and of one's own reading processes		↕		↕	(l) Recognition of implied reader in the text, and the relationship between implied author and implied reader (m) Reflexiveness, leading to understanding of textual ideology, personal identity and one's own reading processes

techniques. The text chosen to be read aloud will likely determine the kinds and frequency of entries to be made.

The listening log, like the reading response journal, enables the English teacher to deepen the authentic and personal response of every student by guiding each one to wider reading and more reflective writing. However, as with other innovative strategies, teachers should beware of the superficial adoption of what appears to be a good idea but becomes nothing more than time-filling practice. It is suggested that the teacher begin with an introductory procedure that will encourage spontaneous but reflective writing. For this activity, a sixty- or ninety-minute period is better than a forty-minute period, which tends to rush the procedure. Nevertheless, both longer and shorter periods have been used successfully. It is also suggested that the teacher use a very short story. Picture books in which the text is not too long lend themselves to this activity. Such stories as Jane Yolen's *The Seeing Stick* and Molly Bang's *Dawn* are ideal. The procedure, typically, is as follows.

The teacher instructs the class:

> I am going to read you a short story. As you listen I want you to reflect on what's going on in your mind. In order to help you, I will read the story in short units and then pause to let you write. The questions I have put on the blackboard are not to be answered one by one. They are suggestions only. They will serve as a guide to what you may write about. Remember this is not a test, and I do not want you to think hard. In fact, my interest is in what comes naturally to your mind as you listen. Other students have found this activity easy and enjoyable. It should be effortless for you. Are there any questions before I begin?

The following are examples of suitable questions to write on the board:

— What's going on in your mind?
— What pictures occur in your head?
— What feelings do you experience?
— What do you expect to happen?
— What questions occur to you?
— What are you thinking about?

As the teacher reads the first portion of the text a hush usually falls over the classroom. Already the narrative seems to cast a spell over the minds and hearts of the students. The teacher reaches the end of the unit, and says simply, "Write."

There are hesitations, blank stares, then a gradual immersion into thinking, composing and writing. The pens and pencils move across the pages. Heads are lowered except to check the blackboard from time to time. Some stop writing far sooner than others. They look around. Others are still engrossed. They stare some more then start writing again.

The teacher might allow five or six minutes for writing this first entry. By this time nearly all will have stopped writing. The one or two who are still composing will have to be stopped. The teacher begins reading again by repeating the last few lines. Then she reads the next unit, stops, and the students recommence writing. As the class proceeds the teacher will be able to lengthen the units read in one stretch. The activity might begin with one page at a time but increase to three pages at a time, which may be more in keeping with the narrative structure.

I have used this procedure with all kinds of classes, always with the same enjoyable results. Students tell me that they like writing about the story.

Most students produce more or less what I expected: a record of the pictures, feelings, hunches, guesses that came to mind as they read. By reading a class set of responses you will learn what you need to know in order to take the next steps in the inquiry process.

There are many variations and possibilities that can be developed. Based on my own experience in about ten different classrooms, I am convinced of the value of the procedure for both curriculum and staff development. What excites me is the potential for co-operative inquiry and development left with the teacher. The procedure offers not only insights into the vast area of how a reader reads (or a listener listens) or how a story works in the mind, but also many challenges to our traditional or "teacherly" preoccupations. But, as always, those matters are left entirely in your hands.

> Each reader builds up a coherent interpretation of a text . . . and each reader will do it differently, because the decisions that have to be made depend to some extent on individual disposition and experience both of the world and of literature. Not only will different readers read the same book differently because their different repertoires of personal and literary experience predispose them to focus on some aspects more than others, but the same reader can never read the same text again the same way.
>
> Jack Thomson

Guiding Students' Booktalk

Aidan Chambers (1985) has prepared a blackboard framework and a general procedure that teachers can use to guide students to explore a text together, as a whole class.

At the end of a reading or listening activity, the teacher gathers the students informally before a blackboard that has four headings and columns as shown in the table below. The teacher asks students to focus on one column at a time and to call out their spontaneous responses in a word or short phrase. Quickly the teacher lists all of the responses the students give, starting with "Likes" and moving on to the other columns in sequence from left to right. The responses usually flow freely under the heading "Likes," and then the pace slows under the other headings. Some words or ideas may appear under more than one heading. Lines can be drawn between entries that do reappear, constructing a web of connections.

Chambers' Framework for Guiding Students' Booktalk

Likes	Dislikes	Puzzles	Patterns

The teacher who adopts this approach should keep several points in mind:

1. This process may be used with the whole class or a small group.
2. The role of the teacher is to guide the students through the process and facilitate the discussion.
3. The students should feel ownership and control of the discussion as they share their feelings, understanding and insights.
4. The process is one of shared discovery that leads the group or the class to deeper levels of understanding, interpretation and appraisal.

2. Extending Responses to the Novel

Transforming Approaches

Currently the novel is the dominant literary genre in our English programs. This is as it should be, for the novel is the most popular form of literary experience in our time. It offers readers an amazing diversity in appeal and personal satisfaction. It is central to the teacher's goal of securing the life-long habit of reading as a most rewarding leisure-time pursuit.

In the past, the presentation of the novel in our classrooms has often proved to be problematic. The novel has been the focus of much labored study and analysis. In some classrooms it still suffers from dull, plodding treatment with questionable outcomes. Moreover, if the course offers the same titles or selections year after year, there is always the danger that the program will become stale and blunted by routine presentation and treatment.

However, there is now available to English teachers a variety of resources, a rich pool of tools and techniques, as well as a profusion of new books and great reads for students in the middle and high-school years. To offer students the best benefits of these current developments, teachers are adopting strategies based on principles of shared reading and collaborative learning.

To begin, teachers work together, as a group of expert readers, to plan and provide a balanced experience of classical, modern and popular works of literature. The collegial inquiry of English teachers usually has three main areas of focus:

• New novels, new authors and treatment of new social issues;

- current developments in literary theory, theories of reader reception and classroom strategies;
- current developments in approaches to collaborative learning, collegial teaching and assessment.

Planning and Providing the Transforming Approaches

When teachers come together to plan the various components or units in their course outlines, they are advised to identify as soon as possible the goals they wish to achieve. Among the questions they may wish to consider when planning the unit on the novel are the following:

- How can we establish classroom conditions that support sustained silent reading?
- How can we implement strategies that actively engage the students in the productive exploration of texts?
- How can we invite students to take ownership and control of their reading, writing and probing responses?
- How can we promote student awareness of the narrative forms of the novel and the literary techniques that authors devise?
- How shall we evaluate the learning outcomes — both the process and the products?

Teachers also need to consider, of course, the selection and organization of books to be included in the various courses. In addressing this concern, some teachers try to maintain a balance between traditional classics, modern classics and the burgeoning body of young adult books or popular paperback fiction. Sometimes, a common theme can be used as an organizing principle. Some common themes that have a strong appeal to adolescents are:

- coming of age;
- death in the family;
- conflict relationships with parents and peers;
- the transition from innocence to experience;
- the rites of passage or initiation into a culture.

Another organizing principle to consider is the approach by genre. Among the more popular genres are: adventure; romance; fantasy; biographical fiction; utopian fiction; mystery; horror; science fiction; and historical fiction.

In addition to considerations of theme and genre, there is the question of the kinds of reading that can be provided:

- the read-aloud experience to share a book with the whole class and to model or demonstrate how to give voice to a text;
- the in-depth reading experience to be shared by students working in small groups on the same book.
- the wide-reading experience to promote individual and independent inquiry.

This chapter outlines several transforming approaches to the novel prepared by different groups of teachers working together, sharing their readings and inquiries and applying what they have selected in order to deliver a balanced and integrated program. Three model approaches are presented:

1. An independent study approach to the classical novel
2. A collaborative approach to the modern novel
3. Two samples of an integrated unit approach using popular paperback fiction related to a theme:
   Theme 1: Things that go Bump in the Night — Horror
   Theme 2: Who We Really Are — The Modern Family

Each of these approaches to the novel is based on collaborative or collegial planning, shared reading by teachers to select and organize a unit, and group and individual response to shared readings in the classroom.

An Independent Study Approach to the Classical Novel

This activity asks initially for an individual response, but then calls for an increasingly collaborative approach.*

Students could be assigned any suitable classical novel, but the following are often popular:

Jane Austen, *Pride and Prejudice*
Charlotte Bronte, *Jane Eyre*
Emily Bronte, *Wuthering Heights*
Joseph Conrad, *Heart of Darkness*
Joseph Conrad, *The Secret Sharer*

---

* This activity was developed by Doug Hilker of Runnymede Collegiate Institute.

William Faulkner, *Light in August*
Thomas Hardy, *The Mayor of Casterbridge*
Thomas Hardy, *Tess of the D'Urbervilles*
D.H. Lawrence, *Sons and Lovers*
Herman Melville, *Moby Dick*
Oscar Wilde, *The Picture of Dorian Gray*

ASSIGNMENT SHEET: INDEPENDENT NOVEL STUDY

1. You will be given two weeks and some class time to read the novel of your choice. While reading, you must keep a reading journal. Divide the novel into ten sections. After each section, write an entry in the journal revealing what thoughts and feelings the novel has aroused in your mind and heart.

2. Select *one* of the following projects:

   (a) Write six or ten diary entries for one of the characters in your novel that reveals his or her secret, personal response to significant events in the novel. The entries should be consistent with the way the character is portrayed in the novel.

   (b) Write a comparison of the role of women in society in the book with their role in society today. How would events in the novel have been different if one woman had acted as she would today? This response should be organized as an essay.

   (c) Rewrite a section of the book from the point of view of a secondary character in the novel. Your character might see him or herself as a central character in the events. Try to make the incident like a short story complete in itself. You may change events in the novel to be consistent with your narrator's knowledge and bias.

   (d) Prepare questions and answers for a TV talk show interview with one of the major characters in your book. If you do this assignment, you will be asked to have another student in the class read the questions you have prepared for the interviewer and to play the part of person being questioned yourself in front of the class.

   (e) With two other students who have read the same book as you, write a script for one of the episodes in the novel and present it for the class.

A SAMPLE ENTRY FROM A STUDENT RESPONSE JOURNAL

Tess of the D'Urbervilles

Entry #10 Chap. 53-59 Sharon V., Gr. 13

My God what a story. I cried more in this last section than I have in all the books I've read before. I can't believe the love which existed between Tess and Angel. It was surely a love of strength and endurance. It was through this love that Angel travelled through Wessex in search of his wife. It was through the same love that Tess killed Alec for all in the past that he had done. It was the love that they both shared which enabled them to find their true selves and their fulfilment.

The elements of this book are so powerful. You can, as I have, feel the joy and pain involved in Tess's life. Hardy is a miraculous writer who has most certainly in this book "put more of his heart than into anything else he ever wrote." You can actually feel the emotion as you read this novel. I've never experienced this feeling in a novel before.

A critic once stated that "no man or woman can read *Tess* sympathetically and not thereafter be of broader mind and more charitable spirit." This statement is indeed true, I don't think I'll ever be the same again. I really love this story.

Tess and Clare found each other once again and through the murder of Alec, became closer than what they could ever be. It was in this period of time that they forgave, loved, cared, grew, shared, matured and became one another. I'm so happy that they found each other again despite the circumstances. I however felt that Alec's death was necessary to bring this book the effect it has. As I heard of Tess murdering Alec, the only thing it proved was her love for Angel. This event was even forgotten as I read on about the two cradled in each other arms.

Tess kept saying how she would rather die than live to see Angel despise her. I admired this quality in her. She would go to the ends of the earth for the man she loved. Izz also told Angel that Tess would lay down her life for him. What love!

The place where Angel and Tess were found was called Stonehenge and it was a heathen temple. This palace of pillars and alters was where Tess and Angel perhaps instinctively knew would be the last place where they would spend time together. She spoke of life after death and if they'd meet again after they died and she also told Angel to take care of LizaLu. It was as if she knew that in the morning this paradise of a few days with her husband would be forever lost and it was.

> The final chapter was the one which spoke of Angel and LizaLu
> venturing up a hill to view the place of their loved one's death. The
> black flag — black symbol of void, death — had moved up the staff
> and blew in the breeze silently.
>
> Tess had finally experienced the happiness that her life had sheltered
> her from in this last section. Being with Angel was her only desire
> and she had got what she desired. I cannot say anything but good
> towards the character of Tess. She has most definitely got to be the
> most intriguing yet simple character of anyone's imagination.

A Collaborative Approach to the Modern Novel*

As with classical novels, teachers may choose any title they think
would be suitable. The following books are among those that
many students enjoy.

Margaret Atwood, *The Handmaid's Tale*
Robertson Davies, *Fifth Business*
Timothy Findley, *Not Wanted on the Voyage*
Timothy Findley, *The Wars*
Joseph Heller, *Catch 22*
John Irving, *The Cider House Rules*
John Irving, *The World According to Garp*
Ken Kesey, *One Flew over the Cuckoo's Nest*
Joy Kogawa, *Obasan*
Margaret Laurence, *The Diviners*
Mordecai Richler, *The Apprenticeship of Duddy Kravitz*
Alice Walker, *The Color Purple*

1. Ask students to form study groups of three. Each group selects
   one novel for study. Throughout the project, the group must
   keep a work journal of each day's activities in a folder. For
   the first four or five classes, assign as homework a number
   of pages or chapters to be read for each class. In class, the
   groups should discuss what happens in the portion read and
   how the author draws attention to what is important in that
   portion. Students should then record their responses as journal
   entries.

---

* This activity was developed by Doug Hilker and Linda Robb of Runnymede
  Collegiate Institute.

2. Ask each member of the group to read an analysis of the novel from reference works in the library and to write a brief report on the main points the author makes. Students may comment on whether they found the library reference analysis helpful or enlightening. Students should be asked to make a correct bibliographic entry of the source at the top of the report.

3. Each group should hand in a one- or two-page written presentation about the novel on *four* of the following topics:
   (a) An analysis of the main character and the significance of that character's experiences as presented in the book
   (b) An analysis of the function of three secondary characters in developing the reader's understanding of the main character or a major theme in the novel
   (c) An analysis of a major theme in the novel and an indication of how it is developed
   (d) An analysis of how symbols are used in the novel to develop character or theme
   (e) An analysis of the role of setting and environment in the reader's understanding of character and theme
   (f) The significance of the title of the novel
   (g) A discussion of two or three social issues raised by the book which the group feels are important

4. Ask each group to prepare three essay questions group members feel test a good understanding of the novel and can be answered in about forty minutes. At the end of the study, set one of these questions for group members to answer.

An Integrated Unit Approach

What is presented here is the result of a collegial process supported by a school district that provided funding for the purpose of curriculum and professional development. All of the teachers involved in the process were teaching in the intermediate or lower grades of large inner-city schools. Among the problems these teachers faced in their classrooms, the following were identified as being of particular concern:

- large numbers of recent immigrants from a diversity of linguistic and cultural backgrounds;
- students from low socio-economic backgrounds, many of whom had either full- or part-time jobs;

- students with low or marginal literacy development and little interest in books or reading;
- some students with learning disabilities, as well as behavioral or psychological disorders.
- many students with a record of academic failure, considered to be potential drop-outs.

The teachers were dissatisfied with their own individual attempts to cope with these problems. However, they were convinced that they could provide more appropriate reading material and thereby elicit a more engaged process of reading, writing and responding in the classroom. After much consultation, research and wide reading in popular paperback fiction, they decided to produce a series of curriculum resource kits, each having a guidebook outlining suggested activities for use. Each kit contained a variety of print and non-print resources selected for their relevance to a common theme. They also designed the following presentation plan for each theme:

1. The teacher reads aloud to the class a novel that not only establishes the theme, but successfully engages students in talking about their own experiences and points of view related to the underlying topic.
2. The teacher displays the collection of core books contained in the kit. These consist of five copies of six selected titles, for a total of 30 books. The students are invited to choose one of the paperbacks provided. Groups or literature circles are formed on the basis of their selection: each group is made up of students who have chosen to read the same title.
3. Response activities are provided to support or guide both group and individual investigation of the novels.
4. Once small group work is in progress, the teacher displays the collection of another 30 to 50 paperbacks, all of which have been chosen by the teachers as having some relevance to the common theme.

The kits have been circulated to the schools by using the existing school district library and courier services. Each kit is used for a three- to four-week period. What follows is the lists of the material resources the teachers selected, together with the suggested response activities:

Theme 1: Things That Go Bump in the Night — Horror

This collection of resources and activities was prepared for use with students at the grade nine level. The theme of horror was chosen on the grounds of its immediate appeal to students who are reluctant readers. However, it is a theme that appeals to a wide variety of students.

READ ALOUD TEXT (TO INTRODUCE THEME OF HORROR)

Rosemary Sutcliff, *Dragon Slayer: The Story of Beowulf* (Penguin).

MULTIPLE COPY TEXTS

All About Monsters (The World of the Unknown Series) (Usborne Publishing).
Raymond Briggs, *Fungus the Bogeyman* (Puffin).
Monsters (Scope Activity Kit) (Scholastic Book Services).
Alice and Joel Schick, *Bram Stoker's Dracula* (Delacourt Press).
Raymond Von Over, *Monsters You Never Heard of* (Tempo Books).

SUPPLEMENTARY READING TEXTS (3 – 5 COPIES OF EACH)

All About Ghosts (The World of the Unknown Series) (Usborne Publishing).
Nina Bawden, *Kept in the Dark* (Puffin).
Daniel Cohen, *Real Ghosts* (Putnam).
Julius Goodman, *The Horror of High Ridge* (Choose Your Own Adventure Series) (Bantam).
Haunted Houses, Ghosts and Spectres (Supernatural Guides) (Usborne Pocket Books).
Steve Jackson and Ian Livingstone, *The Warlock of Firetop Mountain* (Dell).
James Kahn, *Poltergeist* (Warner Books).
Gene Kemp, *The Clock Tower Ghost* (Puffin).
Penelope Lively, *The Ghost of Thomas Kempe* (Dutton).
Georgess McHargue, *Meet the Vampire* (Eerie Series) (Dell Laurel Leaf Books).
R.A. Montgomery, *Vampire Express* (Choose Your Own Adventure Series) (Bantam).
Mysterious Powers and Strange Forces (Supernatural Guides) (Usborne Pocket Books).

Alfred Noyes, illustrations by Charles Keeping, *The Highwayman* (Oxford University Press).

Richard Peck, *The Ghost Belonged to Me* (Dell).

Allen Sharp, *Terror in the Fourth Dimension* (Storytrails Series) (Cambridge University Press).

Allen Sharp, *The Haunters of Marsh Hall* (Storytrails Series) (Cambridge University Press).

Vampires, Werewolves and Demons (Supernatural Guides) (Usborne Pocket Books).

Anne Walsh, *Your Time My Time* (Press Porcupine).

FILMS

Dracula   An edited version of the 1922 German *Nosferatu*, directed by F.W. Fernau. 27 minutes.

The Ghost Belonged to Me   A Walt Disney production based on the book by Richard Peck in which a female ghost is encountered by a young male hero. She alerts him to watch out for a bridge in danger of collapse. 12 minutes.

The Ghost in the Shed   An animated film about a polite ghost who bothers the members of a family until they uncover his bones and give him a decent burial. 10 minutes.

Poltergeist (Video)   Must be obtained from a video shop. This is a feature-length Steven Spielberg film about a ghost who takes a child away from her family and creates havoc.

The assignment sheet for this unit is printed on pages 31 and 32.

Theme 2: Who We Really Are — The Modern Family*

This unit demonstrates the selection of "good reads" available for young people. The theme of the modern family with all its problems and with its differences from the traditional family was chosen by teachers for the grade ten level. Once again, this is a theme that has broad appeal to students at varying levels of ability. Most adolescents have a keen interest in family relationships and the tensions that sometimes arise.

---

* The unit was developed by Heather Bichan and Bonnie Foord of Vaughan Road Collegiate Institute, Doug Hilker of Runnymede Collegiate Institute, and Brenda Protheroe of York Memorial College Institute.

ASSIGNMENT SHEET: THINGS THAT GO BUMP IN THE NIGHT

Activities for Individuals

Write on one of the following topics. Have another student proof-read your work for you. Revise it as necessary and show it to your teacher.

1. Write a letter to the main character of the book saying what you admire about him or her.
2. Write a letter to the author telling him or her what you disliked about the book.
3. Rewrite the ending of the book.
4. Write about an experience you have had which was similar to an experience of one of the characters in the book.

Activities for Group Work

1. Read to the other members of your group a paragraph or two that you found

   — funny
   — painful
   — scary
   — violent
   — mysterious

Tell the group why you thought the passage you read was important to the story.

2. Describe the family in the book you read under the following headings:

   — size of the family (number of people)
   — parents or substitutes
   — siblings
   — who the main character in the family is
   — racial and ethnic origin
   — urban, suburban, or rural
   — pets
   — special aspects of this family

Tell the rest of the group about the family in your novel.
(a) Are any of the families in other books similar?
(b) Do you know of families like the ones described in each book?

3. Profile the main character following the headings below:

— age
— education
— appearance
— special friends
— job experience
— skills
— disabilities
— problems
— strengths
— favorite activities
— health
— family or personal income

Describe your character for the other members of your group.
(a) In what ways are the main characters in other books similar and different?
(b) Which character sounds the most interesting to read about? Why?
(c) Which two characters from different books do you think would get along best
   — in a marriage? Why?
   — on a camping trip? Why?
   — sharing an apartment? Why?

4. Write a poem or a song lyric that illustrates the problem of the main character in your book.
OR
Write and tape a monologue in which the main character in your book explains his or her problem to a very close friend.
Share your poem, song or monologue with the other members of your group.

1. On the diagram, circle the family members who appear in your novel and name them. If there are any family members missing, add them to the diagram. Include, for example, additional brothers and sisters, foster parents and people who replace family members.

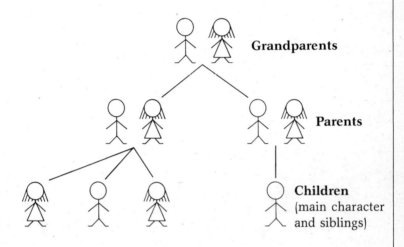

2. (a) Which family member does the main character feel closest to? Explain in one or two sentences.
   (b) With which family member does the main character have the most difficulty? Explain your answer.

3. (a) List the problems of the family.
   (b) Who is responsible for the problems? Explain.
   (c) Tell how they are trying to solve the problems.
   (d) What do you think they should be doing that they are not doing?

4. Describe the situation of the main character at the end of the book. What changes have taken place in the character's family life and in his or her own attitudes and feelings?

3. Storytelling: The Proto-Response*

Teaching How to Tell a Story

The centrality of storytelling to humanity has been well established by such scholars as Harold Rosen, Jerome Bruner and Carol Feldman. The art and promotion of storytelling still occupy a marginal place in many English classrooms. However, these scholars remind us of its importance to cognitive, linguistic, aesthetic and value development of the individual. More recently, Bruner's (1990) research has demonstrated the role of storytelling in developing a sense of self. Many teachers, aware of these developments, have been asking for assistance in this area.

> Storytelling promotes warmth, intimacy and relaxation among people. It can break down racial barriers and bring people to a common essence.
>
> Helen Porter

The following points should be emphasized in teaching students how to tell stories:

1. Storytelling flows from a deep desire to share, the desire to be open about something that has touched one deeply. The choice of story and the manner in which it is told reveals one's

---

This chapter has been adapted from *Once Upon Another Time, A Resource Document on Children's Literature* (Board of Education for the City of York, 1983). The section from which it is adapted was prepared by Helen Porter.

inner self. Although the storyteller may be recreating a traditional tale, it is his or her experience that enters the telling and makes the story ring true.

2. Choose a good story that you enjoy to tell. Your story should have a single theme and a well-developed plot. It should have a brief opening that introduces main characters, sets the scene, arouses pleasurable anticipation and then, almost immediately, plunges into the action of the story.

3. Read the story from beginning to end several times. Read it for pleasure first. Then read it over with concentration. Analyse the story to determine where the appeal lies, what the art form is, what word pictures you want your listeners to see, what mood you wish to create.

4. Read the story aloud and time it. Then tell the story, without reading, and time it again. It should be the same or shorter.

5. Learn the story as a whole rather than in fragments. Do *not* memorize it. Perceive the storyline — the beginning, which sets the stage and introduces the characters and the conflict; the body, in which the conflict builds up to the climax; and the resolution of the conflict. Do not alter the essential storyline.

6. Master the style of the story. To retain the original flavor and vigor of a folk or fairy tale, memorize rhymes or characteristic phrases and songs. Use peculiar words the story might contain.

7. Make the story your own. Become familiar with the characters and the scenes. Build, in your imagination, the setting of the story. How are your main characters dressed? How do they behave? Imagine sounds, tastes, scents, colours. Only when you see the story vividly yourself can you make your audience see it.

8. Be careful of timing. Pause before any change of idea or significant word. Emphasize words that carry meaning. Take poetic passages slowly. Build toward the climax. Use pauses; they can be very effective.

9. Modulate your voice, from whispering to loud. Do not use distracting mannerisms.

As an introductory activity, students could be asked to write reflections on the storytelling process or to create a sketch of an ancient storytelling scene as they imagine it. They should describe how people sit and listen, how the storyteller performs.

At home, the student could pick out a story he or she would like to tell and start to learn it by the method described.

Practical Storytelling Suggestions

Teachers should choose several of the following suggestions.

1. Put the class into small groups. Each group tells a story with each member contributing two or three sentences in turn. Suggestions for opening lines are:
   — When I was five years old, one day I . . .
   — There was an old woman who lived on a hill . . .
   — Once, long ago, the Sun and Moon fell in love . . .
   — The meanest person I ever knew . . .
   The best stories could be told to the whole class by a storyteller from the group.
2. The teacher tells half of a fairy tale, then asks small groups to finish the tale the way they want. Small groups then tell their endings to the large group and compare their choices and decisions.
3. In small groups, students create a tale around one of the following ideas:
   — a deaf and blind boy becoming a world-famous storyteller
   — a young woman becoming a famous explorer, discovering new planets in space
   — a bad baby shaking up a whole town
4. A professional storyteller could be invited to tell stories and talk about the art of storytelling with the class.

Working with Folk Tales

On Narrative: For the delicate probing of inner and outer worlds there is nothing more powerful. And for many of our students — their reader response journals are the evidence — there is nothing more pleasurable.

John Dixon

Folk tales, as the name implies, truly belong to the common people. They exist in many forms and are among the oldest of narratives. Although unnumbered, thousands have been recorded, and many thousands are still part of the oral tradition. The folk tale survives by being told and retold simply because it is worth the telling. It owes its regeneration to the mystical bond that exists between the storyteller and the audience. It is meant to be spoken, heard and even seen.

The distinction between folk tales and fairy tales is sometimes blurred, but there are some characteristics that can be generally ascribed to each type. Folk tales feature common people and animals (rather than heroes, aristocrats and supernatural beings). The animals may have human characteristics or magical powers. The characters can be stereotypical or wildly eccentric, but they are rarely complex, because the folk tale usually moves boldly and quickly.

Many folk tales have a strong didactic or moral tone. There are some striking similarities in theme among moral tales from widely different cultures. For example, tales showing that industry, thrift, ingenuity, honor and kindness are rewarded while sloth, meanness, pride, lust and treachery are punished can be found in cultures as diverse as Oriental and Teutonic, African and Celtic. These folk tales include fables and other animal stories, parables, saints' legends, dilemma tales where the audience is called upon to decide issues, "pourquoi" tales which explain why, and household tales.

Other kinds of folk tales include jests, jokes and merry tales, tricksters' and fools' stories, ghost stories and legends. These are given a strong local and contemporary flavour as they are told, but many themes are sufficiently universal that variations of one tale can be found thousands of kilometres or hundreds of years apart.

The folk tale may be tragic or ribald, riotous or subtle, but it always engages because it has a familiar ring to it — it speaks something of the truth about our values, our fears, our frailties and our triumphs as members of the human family.

Step 1
This step is entirely given over to the students as storytellers.
1. The class is divided into groups, preferably of five or six at the most. Students who have volunteered to prepare and tell a story are assigned to their groups and the storytelling session begins. At the end of the story, each group will want to react, discuss and praise the storyteller. After a brief discussion period, one or more of the following activities may take place:

(a) Students write in their journals about what made the storytelling exciting, what kind of story it was, which part they liked best and so on.

(b) The storytellers switch groups one or more times, each time telling the same story. At the end of this process, the teacher asks the student audiences to discuss the different styles of storytelling they saw, and how much each was influenced by the story and by the storyteller. The teacher asks storytellers to comment on whether or not they made changes in their storytelling as they moved from group to group.

(c) The other students in the group retell stories after hearing the storyteller. This would be spontaneous, rather than rehearsed. How does that change the effect?

2. One student starts a new story with "Once upon a time." He or she takes the story to its first complication, and then stops to allow another storyteller to invent the next part. This process continues until the whole class has finished. Each group member writes down the story as accurately as possible and then tells it to another group or class. The class then discusses the similarities and differences among all the stories that have been produced.

3. If there is an assortment of accents and dialects among class members, students can experiment with the jest or merry tale. Each student in the class chooses a short folk tale from among several provided; nursery tales work well. The students then retell the tale using their own accents or dialects, and adding as many cultural details as possible to make it clearly East Indian, West Indian, Greek, Italian, Canadian, Chinese, Japanese and so on. The critical factor is that *no* student is permitted to imitate — it must be his or her *own* accent, dialect and culture that are used for the tale. This works best if several different versions of the same tale are told.

4. The teacher provides a collection of fool-trickster stories, one per group or one per student. The students learn these stories and then tell them to others during the class (and after class).

Step 2

This step focuses first on animal stories, and then on oral reading as a form of storytelling. Parents often read rather than tell stories to their children and students should be asked to consider the child's *active* participation in this kind of storytelling. The tales in this lesson should be read aloud by the teacher as a demonstration of how lively and dramatic oral reading can be. The teacher should rehearse the reading of two stories. In assembling a wide assortment of animal storybooks, the teacher might consider enlisting the aid of high-school teacher librarian, public-school teachers and teacher librarians, and representatives from bookstores.

1. The teacher reads aloud to the students the two stories prepared.
2. The teacher plays a recording of other animal stories (optional).
3. The students are given ample time to browse through and read from the collection of animal stories that have been made available for this lesson. Each student selects one animal story and, with a partner, rehearses the story for presentation to the group.
4. Presentation of stories to the group is followed by discussion and critique on the performances.
5. Students compare the effect of learning a story in each of the following ways:
   — from a cassette or recording
   — from film and sound
   — from storytelling from memory
   — from a picture book read silently
   — from a picture book read orally

Teachers should try to find one story that can be presented in *all* of these ways, so a fair comparison can be made.

Step 3

This step has several points of focus. It explores the portrayal of humans in folk tales and examines the purpose and validity of stereotyping, which is common in stories.

1. The teacher brings to the class samples of the types of "human" folk tales: parables, pourquoi tales, local legends, stories and so on.
2. Students browse through the stories and select one for presentation as in Step 2.

Working with Fairy Tales

The fairy tale is a rich and profound example of a story. These ancient tales are a part of every nation's memory; passed on from loving older person to child, they are retained as a foundation upon which anyone can build an understanding of how a community and its members interact and develop. Fairy tales and folk tales are the base for a culture's literature.

The fairy tale was told, not read and often changed a little bit with every telling to suit the needs of the child, the teller and the community. They are many versions of Cinderella, The Frog Prince and Rumpelstiltskin, each transformed by the culture it has passed through, but each retaining its essential elements.

There are many reactions to fairy tales today. To some, the stories are too violent; to some, they are too far removed from contemporary life; to some, the stories revive the magic of childhood; and to some, the tales reveal the mystery of the child's unconscious mind. However we look at them, fairy tales are a profound part of the development of our culture and its imagination, and being a multicultural community we have a treasure of wonderful stories to share.

Step 1

1. The class sits in a semicircle with the storyteller's chair in a central position. The teacher may like to have the room darkened and candles lit for dramatic effect during the telling of the stories. This device helps to free the teller to be more dramatic with voice and gesture.
2. As an introduction the teacher may give a definition of the fairy tale. A fairy tale is a story that has:
   (a) magical occurrences;
   (b) supernatural beings — dwarves, giants, trolls, fairies and transformed animals;
   (c) a main character who must resolve a problem that impedes development and that, once resolved, leads to maturity;
   (d) a happy ending.

   A brief discussion of the differences and similarities between folk tales and fairy tales may be held.
3. The teacher, who has memorized two or three fairy tales, can then take the teller's chair and, with the room darkened and candles lit, tell a tale to the class. Possible stories include:

- The Frog Prince
- Rumpelstiltskin
- Hansel and Gretel
- Cinderella
- Little Red Riding Hood

4. Students are asked to find or remember their favorite tales and bring them to the next class.

Step 2

The students, with their favorites prepared, may take the chair and tell several stories.

Step 3

1. Library staff members are asked to pull out books that include fairy tales.
2. In the library, groups of four or five students can sit around small tables and look at, read and tell the fairy tales that are found in the books that have been pulled out.
3. Students could be asked to discuss illustrations, what supernatural creatures may look like or where they may have come from and the visual aspects of the stories. The teacher might then ask students to illustrate tales, make puppets, cook up gingerbread houses, design castles or draw maps of the journeys involved in the stores.

   Students should be encouraged to use resources other than just books of fairy tales. Other possibilities include:
   - books on supernatural creatures such as giants, trolls, dwarves, fairies, witches, transformed animals, half-human beast
   - books on castles or medieval villages, architecture and furniture
   - films or videos presenting fairy tales
   - records and tapes of fairy tales being told

Step 4

In small groups, the students could take a favorite tale and analyse it, illustrate it, modernize it, make a puppet play of it for a kindergarten class, change it to suit another culture or technology (e.g., space-age technology) or learn it to tell to someone specific.

The teacher should participate equally with the students and discuss the delights or problems presented by the projects and the tales themselves.

4. Response to Poetry

Poetry: From Sound to Meaning

There has emerged in our traditional treatment of poetry in the classroom a widespread belief that poetry is difficult, esoteric or obscure; that, unless a teacher is "specialized" in analytical skills and literary theory, it should be approached with a great deal of caution. The following suggestions are offered as a means of dispelling these popular misconceptions as well as providing some support for non-specialist teachers.

An informal approach that employs an everyday provision of aural experience is authentic, for it allows the poem to speak for itself. Reading poetry aloud to the class, giving voice to the signs on the page are themselves acts of interpretation. How should this poem be spoken or performed? The answer to this question is one a teacher can both model and explore. Listening to poems, presenting poems, preparing the presentation of poems — all of these are productive, whole-language approaches involving process, product, code, content and behavior. The teacher who provides and sustains such activity is truly a regenerative teacher: regenerative of program, of self, and of students and students' attitudes toward poetry.

Providing a Listening Experience of Poems

The following activities provide a good range of listening experiences:

1. A poem is read without discussion every day for a week, by the teacher or by a student who has prepared the reading.

Literature is produced by, and appeals to, the imagination. The imagination is a creative and constructive power: it is different from reason, though it is intelligent, and different from feeling, though it is sensitive. If we are responding to someone else's poem, we should respond to it at first with intelligence and feeling, as we do to anything else outside ourselves. But sooner or later we come up against the questions of how our own powers of creation can be related to whatever the poet has made. For, however unlikely it is that we could make anything like *King Lear* or *Paradise Lost*, our response even to that level of creation still has in it some quality of recognition. Lear, on the heath is not like anything we have actually experienced, either in waking life or in dreams. Nevertheless he reminds us that besides actual worlds and fantasy worlds, we do have an imaginative world of our own, a world of possibilities, so to speak, and that Lear is within range of something that we can imagine. We know very little about our own imaginative worlds; even a great genius may not know much about what his genius is producing. Hence, we are, at least at first, totally inarticulate about what we can imagine, until something in literature, say a poem, comes along and expresses it. Then we realize that the poem corresponds to something in a world that we have lived in and lived with, but knew nothing about until the poem spoke for us.

Northrop Frye

Individual exploration of the poem may or may not follow. Each student keeps a record tracking each day's insights. These could be stated at the end of the week.

2. Students prepare a taped reading of a poem. Alternatively, with the help of other students and staff members (voices beyond the class), they prepare several readings of the same poem.

3. The class listens to a taped or live (or both) reading of a poem. In a period of silence following, students jot down instant reactions to ponder later, when they begin to develop personal responses to the poem.

4. Working in a small group, one student reads a portion of the poem and then passes the book on to the next student, who continues with the next portion. This process is repeated until the entire poem has been read and listened to several times. Each member of the group will listen more than read.

5. Several pairs of students prepare a reading of the same poem. The readings by each pair are heard, compared and assessed.
6. The teacher reads a poem, or plays a taped reading of it (prepared by teacher or student). Working in pairs, students write brief instant reaction notes and exchange them. The poem is read (or played) again and further notes or comments are added. Class discussion follows. Such presentations can easily be modified or adapted with almost limitless variation. The teacher, with research, will develop a repertoire of presentational strategies.
7. Paul Fleischman has composed poems in two columns to be read aloud by two readers at once, as in a musical duet (*I Am Phoenix: Poems for Two Voices*. Harper & Row, 1985). Students enjoy performing them.
8. The teacher directs the class in a choral reading. The text of the poem could be displayed (at first) on an overhead projector. Music or sound effects (live or taped) could be appropriately added. A tape-recorder is useful during rehearsals to foster the class's critical refinement of their own performance.

Sustaining Wide Reading and Inquiry

Classroom Anthologies

One of the best activities to sustain inquiring and searching reading of poems is the making of anthologies. Once more students work in pairs, in small groups or as individuals contributing to a classroom anthology and/or individual or small group anthologies. Many schools and English departments have stored away in their bookrooms class sets of published collections, perhaps worn out or outmoded for various reasons. In addition, many school libraries have extensive collected works of various poets and expensive volumes, such as *The New Oxford Book of English Verse*. In any event, what is needed is about 50 different hardcover and paperback collections of poetry, organized along different lines.

These are released to the class for purposes of browsing and searching to find those pieces that have strong appeal for the various individuals or groups. Under teacher guidance the students can decide the methods of selecting and organizing chosen poems: by topic, theme, genre or form, mode, setting or whatever. The students choose their own criteria and methods of publishing or displaying the poems. Skills in graphic design, calligraphy, collage, montage and photography are used to produce a well-crafted anthology complete with cover and table of contents.

Poem Posters

A variation on the classroom anthology is the preparation of poem posters using appropriate design and graphic art to set off or illumine the text. The posters are displayed for a short period of time in the classroom or in display areas in the school.

Activities to Promote Close, Careful and Attentive Reading

1. Several poems are typed up or copied out with certain words missing. Working in pairs or groups, students are asked to choose the best word to fit in. The teacher may choose to omit words that will draw attention to a chosen feature — e.g., rhyme, rhythm, imagery, pattern or structure.
2. Several poems without titles are presented to the class (one per group). Each group prepares a title and passes it on to the next group. Later class discussion considers the optional titles, and may lead to a consensus.
3. Each group of students is presented with an envelope containing a poem that has been typed out and cut into parts. The students open the envelope and spread out the parts. They then decide on the best sequence of parts. When they have agreed, they copy it out and exchange envelopes with another group. Later the groups compare sequences chosen. Of course, not all poems lend themselves to such cutting, but this activity emphasizes structural features that might otherwise be neglected.
4. Various words are inserted into a typed version of the poem. Working in pairs or groups, students are asked to identify and replace the inserted words. Comparisons with authentic texts may follow.
5. Pupils attempt a parody or create an opposite effect by making substitutions as in poems such as Ezra Pound's "Winter is a-coming in" or Hiebert's "Tree Fever." Marlowe's "Passionate Shepherd to His Love" and Raleigh's "The Nymph's Reply" are good models as well.

Student Presentational Readings or Prepared Performances

There are many advantages to the practice of assigning small groups to prepare a poem for presentation to class. Conducting presentations ensures that the experience of poetry is not only lived through, but also refined, by rehearsing and decision making in collaboration with others. The presentation process requires the group to invent a sub-text, or context, to enlarge on the experience of the individual reading. It moves the motionless drama in the mind out into a moment of drama in the classroom.

By this dramatizing process the students are led to discover latent meanings and nuances in the text, and thereby to establish stronger links with their own personal experience, beliefs, feelings and insights. Moreover, small group presentations are a good antidote to what Patrick Dias (1987) has called the "full frontal approach with the teacher at the head of the class directing the reading and interpretation of the poem for the class." In this traditional approach, it is the teacher's voice and authority that are being exercised. With the student presentation approach, the student's voice, imagination and interpretation are developed in an authentic and empowering way.

Depending on the needs of the class and the level of instruction, the teacher may choose between two variations of this method: each group could present a different poem, or each group could present the same poem. In either case the group decides the manner of presentation: live or taped and, if taped, audio or video cassette. The presentation may involve one, or more than one, speaker/actor; it may be a choral reading or a dramatization with appropriate use of props and musical accompaniment. Sometimes a group may choose to project a series of images using either a slide or overhead projector. Sometimes it may be appropriate to move out of the classroom to a gym, cafeteria, auditorium, corridor space or even outdoors. The onus is always on the group presenting to reconstruct or represent their interpretation of the text or even an extension of their shared understanding. The onus is on the rest of the class to assess and to critique their performance positively.

Small Group Investigation of Poetry

In the response-based approach, small group investigation of teacher-assigned poems is the central process in the "teaching" of poetry, in all grades and levels of instruction. With the use of simple procedures outlined below, the teacher can transform a classroom full of individual and divergent views and opinions into truly collaborative groups, totally engaged in negotiating the meaning and intention of a poem by incorporating aspects of form, structure and imagery. In addition, the teacher establishes a pleasant and productive experience enjoyed by all interpretive communities. There is no better way to meet the needs of students who may have acquired negative attitudes and beliefs about poetry as a result of previous traditional study of poems.

Characteristic of small group investigation is reading it out, talking it through, writing it down, and at times (as suggested above) rehearsing for acting it out or presenting to the class. Here is one excellent description of the basic procedure which, when mastered, can be modified, adapted or improved upon as each teacher deems appropriate to match the needs of different classes. This procedure is taken from *Making Sense of Poetry: Patterns in the Process* (Patrick Dias, 1987).

1. Groups are formed. A leader for each group is chosen and given the responsibility for chairing the discussion and reporting the group's account of the poem. Group members take turns at chairing discussion sessions.
2. Copies of the poem are distributed. The teacher reads the poem.
3. A student reads the poem. The teacher determines from the reading probable sources of misunderstanding caused by syntax or unfamiliar words.
4. The teacher invites inquiries about meanings of unfamiliar words and assists without directing interpretation. Students are encouraged to respond to such inquiries; but this stage of dwelling on words even before the context has emerged should not be drawn out.
5. The students read the poem aloud within their groups, and then again silently. Within the group each student is expected to state *in turn* an initial reaction, feeling or observation occasioned by the reading. The students do not remark on one another's responses until each member of the group has shared an initial response. (This is an important stage in the process and should be strictly followed. Some individuals cannot wait to confront others and, if they are articulate, overwhelm reticent members of the group, who are likely to forget what they were going to say.)
6. Following this preliminary round of comment, the students

are no longer required to speak in turn and they may comment freely on what they have just heard and share observations in their endeavor to make some sense of the poem. One means of keeping the discussion going is to have the students read in turn a sentence or stanza at a time, commenting as they go along. This allows the students to interrupt with comments and questions as they build up their sense of the poem. It also helps the group to establish the text of the poem — what is and is not present in the text.

7. Whenever an impasse is reached in discussion, the students are encouraged to return to the text of the poem.

8. Half way through the discussion, and also near the end of the group discussion, the students are encouraged to reread the poem in the light of new information that has emerged.

9. Near the end of the discussion (20-25 minutes before it needs to come to a close), one member in each group rereads the poem aloud. The members of the group consider any meanings that have emerged and prepare an account that represents their experience of the poem, which is to be shared with the large group. At all times the teacher's concern is not to influence the form and content of this account. Students should be discouraged from taking written notes.

In a larger group session students usually report in turn for their groups. After the first group has reported, the onus is on each subsequent reporter to build on the previous account, agreeing and disagreeing, and reporting any new insights that have occurred in the process. Members of the group supplement their reporters' accounts of the poem if they feel the need to, and record minority opinions.

10. The several accounts of the poem should create the impression that the poem is much more than each of the summary accounts has made out. It remains for the teacher to raise questions that arise from the discussions and the groups' reports, to help relate some of the several strands in the groups' reports, to introduce, where useful, the terminology that helps the class make sense of and place their observations. During this wrap-up the teacher should at all costs avoid creating the impression that group members do not have the resources within themselves to deal adequately with the poem, and that the teacher is the ultimate arbiter of the poem's meaning. The questions that are raised by the teacher at this

concluding stage must be real questions sparked by student interest and inquiry, and reinforcing students' beliefs in their own resources as readers.

SMALL GROUP INVESTIGATION: AN ALTERNATIVE PROCEDURE

Doug Hilker, English Department Head at Runnymede Collegiate Institute, describes an alternative approach to small group investigation of poetry.

The idea is simple. Each student reads the poem and writes down three questions about it that he or she would like answered. Then students select a partner, try to answer each other's questions and arrive at three questions about the poem they still would like more ideas about. In the next step, two sets of partners join together in a group of four, and answer each other's questions. They settle on *one* question they will present for full class discussion.

When I used this method on Margaret Atwood's "Progressive Insanities of a Pioneer" and Don McLean's "Vincent," I was very impressed with the quality of questions and discussion at each stage of the process. Final discussion about the Atwood poem centred on the structure of the poem, on whether the country being discussed was Canada and on the conflict between the human need for order and nature's habit of overgrowing and knocking down human constructs. With "Vincent," final discussions focussed on the poet's purpose in writing the poem, on the conflict between artist and audience in many art forms and on the role of the artist in society. Not a bad level of discussion at all!

The beauty of the approach is the level of involvement by the students. They're all interested — after all, they are discussing their own questions. They all play the role of questioner and answerer. In many ways, I felt the classes went further and deeper than if I had asked all the questions.

At the end of class the students wrote about the poems, the ideas generated in their discussions, and the process in which they were involved. It was some of the most interesting spontaneous writing of the year.

Ryder Payne, English Department Head at George Harvey Collegiate Institute, suggests snowballing — building from individual reaction to group response and from limited meanings to a broad range of interpretations.

1. Put the following text on the blackboard or an overhead:

> Listening . . .
> After a while,
>   I take up my axe again.*

2. Ask the students to list in silence as many meanings as they can find for this poem — for example,
   - a butcher listening to the radio before resuming meat cutting
   - a lumberjack listening to the song of the whitethroat before continuing to cut down trees

3. In pairs, students compare meanings and add any new ones they can discover together — for example,
   - a psychopath listening to see if her victim is asleep before attacking
   - a firefighter listening for sound of trapped people, then resuming his rescue efforts
   - a rescuer listening for the cries of people buried by an earthquake, before cutting away at the debris

4. Pairs join with two other people to form groups of four. They compare meanings, then see if more can be discovered through discussion — for example,
   - a camper preparing a fire, listening to the sounds of nature before countinuing to cut firewood
   - a frustrated student, having listened to the teacher talking for the past 20 minutes, entertaining thoughts of violence
   - "axe" is slang for a guitar: a musician listening to her recording and then resuming playing
   - an executioner listening to the prayers of a priest before going about his job of cutting off the heads of aristocrats (could even be the man who executed Anne Boleyn, Mary Queen of Scots or Charles I)

5. All groups share their different meanings with the rest of the

---

* By Rod Wilmot, From B. Kellow and J. Kriksat, *Poetry and Language* (McGraw-Hill Ryerson, 1983).

class. The teacher introduces the notions of symbol and metaphor, and the class seeks other means — for example,
- Minister of Finance preparing his budget
- a debater listening to her opponent, then presenting her own arguments (grinding her own axe)
- Jack the Giant Killer listening to the approaching giant and preparing to hack through the beanstalk

Poetry Writing: Points of Departure*

The ways of encouraging students to write poetry are as diverse as the subjects, styles and forms of expressive composition. The suggestions made below are not exhaustive; they are, in fact, just a beginning. Listening to what students talk about and being aware of what students notice will enable teachers to multiply the number of suggestions made here. Nor should these suggestions be considered prescriptive. Teachers will see the need for re-wording, adapting and transforming these procedures to meet the interests of the students they are encouraging.

Long periods are helpful for pre-writing activities, paired criticism, discussion, proofreading and revision; in short, for all the activities that are important in the poetry-writing process. Teachers with less time available may need to adjust some suggestions to fit their time limits.

General Principles for Poetry Writing Activities

1. Assign a poetry project to be completed over a long period of time, rather than nightly assignments. This allows for considerable discussion and revision of all the poems worked on. It also allows a student to drop a poem that is not working out successfully. It is a good idea to ask for *all* notes and preliminary work to be handed in (and to evaluate it in terms of effort) as well as finished poems.
2. Students should be allowed to deviate from the focus of the assignment, especially if they can give interesting reasons for wanting to do so. Since the assignment is mainly something to get them started, it would be foolish to let the assignment itself become a stultifying bone of contention.

* This section has been adapted from *Write Out of Your Life*, a resource unit prepared by Gary Hophan of Weston Collegiate Institute.

3. Much of the early critical work and appreciative commentary can be done in pairs. Students working in this way are less likely to feel shy or inhibited.
4. The teacher should allow writing to connect with talk. The more discussion of ideas, images, metaphors, diction and tone, the better. It is best for the teacher to stay out of this discussion as much as possible: students *will* talk about the metaphors their classmates have used, for instance, but they will probably do so best in their own words and without recourse to literary terminology.
5. The teacher should stress importance of note-taking prior to writing. The more precisely sense impressions are noted, the more useful they will be as a poem is being written. Notes written in phrases will be more helpful than lists of single words. It is also important that notes be thorough: the more complete one's notes, the greater the possibilities for selecting and combining.

Pre-Writing Activities

1. *Paintings* and *photos* (reproductions, photos, slides, filmstrips) are good jumping-off points for descriptive poetry and expressive prose, especially for students unable as yet to "read" real-life scenes. Students should take notes on:
   (a) what they see (sizes, shapes, colours, numbers, etc.);
   (b) other sensations (hearing, touching — they can imagine what they would experience were they in the scene);
   (c) comparisons ("the old lady's face looks like that of a monkey");
   (d) inferences ("must be at least a hundred years ago");
   (e) mood and feeling of the scene.

   When the teacher is satisfied that notes have been taken thoroughly and seriously, he can have the students re-work their material into poetic form.
2. Students can be asked to study a *place*, making precise notes on people, buildings, sounds, smells, all of the sense impressions they experience. Point-form commentaries on moods and ideas can also be written. Since most students should be able to produce voluminous notes for this assignment, the writing of a poem will require careful selection and organization, and these skills will be sharpened.

3. Students can be asked to bring to school any *objects* that they find interesting. Objects should be fascinating in visual and/or tactile ways, and should have significant personal associations. Notes should be taken on the objects themselves as well as on the associations. Material from the two sets of notes combine to make a poem.

4. Students are interested in other *people* and will quite willingly (at any age) take notes on the appearance and personality of those they meet. Students will also be able to take useful notes on a person's environment. Imagination will provide suitable specific settings for people not normally seen outside of school. The presentation of a character can be the purpose of a poem shaped from all of these notes. Another possibility is to have the character deliver an interior or dramatic monologue. This choice requires the student to create an appropriate voice for another person, to ''get out of herself'' to some extent. A variation on the monologue is the writing of an epitaph for one's character or allowing him to speak from the grave, in the manner of *Spoon River Anthology*.

5. *Monologuing* is an easy bridge from literary study to expressive writing. Many students who are unable to write essays that adequately express their response to what they've read *are* able to monologue (in prose) the characters they've become interested in. Since the writing of monologues from literature is a fairly common part of novel and drama study, no examples are included here. Below, however, is an example of what can happen when a student combines an understanding of a character with her own thought.

THE LAMENT OF THE MAIDEN OPHELIA

Oh! How they suffer, those too soft and sweet:
— they break like brittle windowpanes
under a summer storm's relentless hail.
Pelted or laid open to the four winds
they break: the pieces fall upon a cold, hard bed,
and there remain forgotten until swept away by Time.

You wonder at my words, and stare blank into my face
as though trying to find the root of just insanity
mirrored in my eyes.
How placidly you sit there, silently condemning me as mad
I am mad: driven insane from too much trust and innocence
driven to drab despair from the very man I love. Oh,

to think man's greatest organ of all, the mind,
can be reduced to clay so quickly by another man.
And then there is woman; whose mind and body and soul
seem to have been cast in fate to be forever
manipulated by man.

Oh! How they suffer! With their bloom and nuance of mystery
like violets, plucked too quickly:
And then, once wilted at the very edges,
they are thrown into the river,
washed away into a flow of countless sisters' tears.

Renata B.
(Grade 13)

6. An activity that can lead either to monologue or to descriptive poetry is to ask the students to think of *disguises* they would assume if they were going to live incognito for a time. Students should have five minutes to decide on a persona, and then they should be asked to list the transformations that would be needed to effect the disguise. When all have written notes, they can begin to write a poem that focusses on, or is spoken from the point of view of, this new identity. What most students end up doing, sometimes unconsciously and therefore without inhibitions, is to concoct a metaphor for the self. Invariably there is an interesting connection between the disguise chosen and the personality of the student. The students understand and say much more about themselves than about the chosen persona, be it a fortune teller, cab driver or whatever. Below is a poem produced in response to this assignment.

HIDDEN THOUGHTS

She whirls around on stage
The lights they flicker like fireflies.

The cameras, they click like the thoughts
that no one hears.
They flash through her mind, but she
dare not let them stay.

Dressed always in the newest of fashion.
A smile painted shiny on her lips.
A complexion as soft as down.
Fingernails as sharp as the thoughts
that stab like blinding light.

By day she smiles, she lives with illusions
By night she cries and lives in truth. .
All alone, all lights turned out, no more
painted smiles, left alone.
Alone with thoughts that stab like
blinding light.

Pamela B.
(Grade 10)

7. *Personal experience* is the starting point for most student poetry of quality. Students can be asked to write a paragraph (which no one else need read) that expresses a deep personal wish or fear or that recalls a meaningful memory. They should then be told to make their writing more suitable for public consumption by rendering it into poetry. Students may wish to share their paragraph work in pairs and discuss suggestions for their poems. When poems are finished, some should be read aloud. Students will come to appreciate that poetry centred on personal experience will connect with others, either on a literal level or by analogy. A sense of how literary symbolism works may begin to develop, as in the following example.

ROOM FOR RENT

A space for vacancy
which no one can fill.
A lonely spot
a missing link,

Suddenly times are changed,
members open doors,
someone comes in,
and everything is rearranged.

Why did she come
to fill this space?
Was it loneliness we had to face?
Without a regret,
she walked in,
me with revenge
on my face.

She did not stop
she abruptly took over;
must I move on, and
forget the past?

Is it wise to cover up before,
and open the door
which will not fill me,
but leave me empty?

Jim B.
(Grade 10)

5. Creative Engagement with Children's Books, Picture Books and Shakespeare

Children's Literature

The introduction of a unit on children's literature has proved to be one of the more exciting and rewarding innovations in secondary school English programs in recent years. Among the objectives of the unit may be listed the following:

- a rediscovery of the delights of the books and the stories of our childhood and the powerful memories and experiences associated with them;
- an introduction to the amazing realm of children's literature today;
- an exposure to some of the main writer/illustrators of children's literature today, their works and their views;
- an obvious link-up with media literacy, visual arts and values in education;
- the creation of a children's storybook;
- students' presentation of their stories to primary-school children in neighborhood schools;
- a discovery by young adults, who may soon be parents, of the value of reading to infants and toddlers and the provision of some familiarity with the impressive range and diversity of books suitable for young children.

For those unfamiliar with what has come to be questionably designated as children's literature, there is no convincing argument for including it in secondary schools. For those who have

> More and more our students' parents and even our own friends and acquaintances outside the field of English teaching think of literature as a specialized body of academic material that is "covered" in school and afterwards forgotten.
>
> Robert Scholes

discovered the rich diversity of this amazing realm, no argument is necessary. Delight is always its own defence.

The doors to this realm are just beginning to open, allowing for a wise selection of picture books. Of course, young adults wouldn't be caught dead walking down the halls of their schools carrying what appears to be a book for babies. But within the security of their own classrooms many are fully engrossed in reading something they can manage and enjoy. In some cases they claim that they are just rehearsing a reading of the book in order to read it to a younger brother or sister at home, or to the kid they are baby-sitting tonight or even to a primary class in the neighborhood school. And, indeed, these are sometimes among the incentives used by teachers to get students to look at a book they will enjoy. Moreover, when they have the opportunity to read to a real audience, they enjoy modelling teacher or adult behavior.

Procedures for Getting Started

1. Taking turns in small groups, students share nursery rhymes or finger games they can remember from their childhood. Much hilarity follows, as memories are triggered quite spontaneously. The purpose here is to set a relaxing tone for the sharing of personal memories.
2. Still in groups, the students retell spontaneously any stories they remember from their childhood. These stories may have been told or read to them.
3. The students make up their own children's stories spontaneously. Working in groups, they are given a line to get them started — a line such as, "A long, long time ago a man built a house in the woods." One person starts the story off by repeating the line and adding whatever occurs to him. The next person takes over when he falters, and the process continues around the group until everyone has a turn or the story comes to a conclusion. Students then use another primer, such as,

61

"There once lived a lad down by the sea." The purpose here is to let the imagination flow into words, and words into narrative events. Students use each other's ideas, they support each other and they experience collaboration in storytelling.

4. Next the groups are asked to recall a favorite fairy tale or legend from childhood. At this time they are asked to retell the story by reinventing or substituting one aspect, such as the setting, gender of the central character, point of view or outcome. Once they catch the idea they begin to rehearse and to write out their stories. These written drafts are completed for homework. In the follow-up lesson they share their stories.

5. If teachers are familiar with the techniques of the fantasy journey, this is a good time to take students on an inner journey into their own minds where they reconstruct a possible world of wonder and imagination. When they return from their journeys they write about them.

6. The next assignment requires the students to bring to class several children's books, new or old. Some students still have their favorite books at home. Others will have to visit the children's department of the public library or make a visit to the resource centre in the neighborhood junior school. It is wise for the teacher to have on hand some examples of high quality picture books. These can be borrowed from board resources, such as the elementary school libraries or the public libraries, or, if possible, purchased from a book store. Once again the class will be quite excited when they all arrive with their favorite children's books. To get on with the task at hand, students are put back into groups where they each prepare at least one story to read aloud to the group, and then lead a discussion on the main features of the book, including cover, format, illustrations, narrative style, use of patterns, images, symbols and so forth.

7. All of the foregoing steps have been a lead-up to the major assignment for this unit: namely, the production of a storybook to be presented to a live audience in one of the primary grades of the feeder or elementary schools in the neighborhood. Generally, elementary school principals are quite receptive to visitors, especially older students working under teacher supervision for the completion of a storytelling or book-sharing unit. Some teachers prefer to arrange several visits. On the

first visit the students have a chance to observe, listen to and work along with primary children in order to become familiar with their world, their language and their response to stories, as well as the kind of stories that appeal to them and those that should be avoided.

On the second visit, the students come prepared to read to the children or to tell a story. The third visit is left for the students' presentation of their own stories to the children.

If the assignment is presented during a whole-class discussion, the students can share in deciding on such questions as:

— whether to work individually, in pairs or trios
— whether or not to form author/illustrator partners
— whether or not to seek help from illustrators in art classes
— which method of book development or creation to use — storyboard, substitution or original creation
— what will be the time lines for completion of the story and for visits to the primary grades

Once the decisions about the assignment are made and are clear to the class, the teacher then can move on to another unit, allowing for a two- to three-week interval for the completion of the story.

On the day decided, the students bring to class their original masterpieces. Once again the excitement builds as intensive book-swapping gets under way. Some arrangements should be made for the display of the books and for the presentation of the stories to the class before students go out to the primary grades.

In classrooms where the above procedure is followed, with resourceful adaptation as required, the results are most rewarding for all concerned: for the students, for the primary-school children and for the teachers who must evaluate both the process and the product. As with no other assignment, storybook making engages some students in a sustained effort for long hours and on weekends. The effort, ingenuity and imagination they bring to the task are amazing.

For many young adults the reading of their stories to primary grade children is one of the most rewarding and affirming experiences of their maturing years.

Picture Books: A Powerful Medium

Within the classrooms of some progressive and enthusiastic teachers, picture books have found a valid place. Often, however, the books are used only in conjunction with a unit on children's literature or as models for picture-book making by senior students. There are very few, if any, picture book collections in our secondary school libraries, or if there are, they may be on a shelf marked "E" for "easy." But a picture book shelf deserves the designation "E" for "everybody." Contemporary picture books, the variety or genre being promoted here, offer a distinctive aesthetic and literary experience by constructing a dialogue between the picture and the word, between the icon and the text. The power of the picture book lies in its inescapable charm that beguiles the readers/viewers into a deepening experience within their own dialogic imagination.

What is the rightful place of the contemporary picture book in our Language Arts–English program? How can it be secured?

For teachers, the perception of picture books may be shaped by childhood experience of them. For parents, perception of picture books may be related to book-sharing experiences with children at home. In general, we tend to consider the use of picture books as most appropriate for children — for emergent or beginning readers. The excitement of the visual displays affords an easy prop for the minimal print or text.

The visual props may work for struggling beginners but sensitive teachers may hesitate to confront robust adolescents with something that seems suitable only for babies.

Such considerations actively prevent us from discovering the present sophisticated transformations taking place in picture book production. Anyone familiar with the recent work of Ted Hughes, Raymond Briggs, Charles Keeping, Jane Yolen, Molly Bang and Chris Van Allsburg, for example, would recognize that the picture book genre has become what David Lewis (1990) calls "the most extraordinary and innovative of literary and artistic forms." In order to help us overcome our shared blindness or prejudice toward picture books, Lewis explains the parallels he sees between post modernism in adult literature and the contemporary picture book. With the help of writers and critics such as David Lewis and David Lodge, we have at our disposal an exciting and enthusiastic introduction to some of the more oblique or esoteric developments in literary theory. What Lodge has done for deconstructionism, Lewis is attempting for contemporary picture books —releasing us from our own prejudices, and shedding new light on metafictive concerns.

In her insightful booklet *How Texts Teach What Readers Learn*, Margaret Meek (1988:40), concludes with the following observations:

> For more than five years my colleagues and I examined the reading of a group of adolescents who had been deemed to be unteachable. In fact they had learned too well too many unhelpful lessons. They had never been trusted with real texts. Their early encounters with reading had not included books as a source of pleasure, play, desire. At best they could say a few words after prompting. They had been given only conditional entry into their culture and they wanted nothing of the tyranny of literacy. We gave them real books and showed them how texts teach.

Among the real books Meek and her colleagues gave to these "unteachable" adolescents were picture books — a source of "pleasure, play, desire."

For three reasons — recent transformations in picture book production, recent developments in the teaching of literacy and new insights in literary theory — the place and use of picture books in the secondary school curriculum should be secure. But it isn't! What will it take to make sure that we "find ways of examining and studying the articulation of word and image in this most extraordinary and innovative literary and artistic form" (Lewis, 1990).

Any one familiar with recent developments in the elementary school curriculum will be well aware that children's books, especially picture books, are being restored to their rightful place in the reading, writing, drama and visual arts programs. Many school districts and, increasingly, many schools are holding annual young authors' conferences. In some areas parents are taking an active part by the running of book-making centres.

What is really amazing in all this book-centered activity is the degree of engagement, of craft, of competence and of imagination displayed by students. For the promotion of literacy in schools, book making has become a powerful, pleasurable vehicle. It is an ideal medium for the integration of language arts, dramatic arts, visual arts, values education and media literacy.

What is being initiated and nurtured in our elementary schools should be extended and developed in our senior and secondary schools. The place of picture books should be linked to the following objectives:

- providing an authentic experience of contemporary literature — verbal and visual;
- providing models of excellence in crafting books;
- providing successful reading experience to young adults in basic programs, experience that would not otherwise be available to them;
- promoting the retelling (or re-writing) of traditional folk and fairy tales within a new frame or context;
- providing exciting book-sharing experiences;
- promoting storybook-making in the intermediate and senior divisions.

Providing an Interactive Experience of Picture Books

Teachers should begin by giving themselves some preparation time to become familiar with recently published picture books. It is important at this stage for readers to discover for themselves the richly rewarding aesthetic experience that is offered to the reader/viewer of each book. In addition, teachers should allow themselves adequate time to select and collect those books which merit their students' attention. As a rule of thumb, teachers need to browse through about 100 books in order to select 30. As a result, it's a good idea for colleagues to work on the process together, as long as enthusiasm is shared and everyone involved is willing to visit public libraries and children's book stores, and to consult guides to children's literature.

The resulting display of about 30 well-selected picture books will transform the environment of a typical secondary school classroom. The teacher should be ready for the excitement the books will stimulate.

The teacher may want to provide some preliminary activity to focus the students' attention and to establish a tone for the new venture. The students could be asked to sit in groups of four. They would then recall a favorite book — picture book, or story-book — from childhood and retell the story to a partner. Next, they would follow the procedure outlined below.

1. Working in pairs, within the group of four, students decide which partner will go to the display and select one book.
2. In pairs, students share the reading and viewing of the book in their own way and at their own pace. The teacher should allow about 20 minutes for this stage.
3. When students have finished the reading/viewing, they decide which partner will retell the story. The storyteller rehearses with the partner, either using the book or not using it, as he or she sees fit.
4. When both sets of partners have rehearsed the retelling, then the storytellers take turns in presenting pieces to the other partners in the group of four.

By following such a procedure, with suitable modifications, the teacher will engage the students in a process in which about 12 to 16 books are shared simultaneously. The process may be repeated over several sessions so that each group has the experience of sharing about 8 to 10 different books.

Any variety of activities could follow. The students themselves may make spontaneous suggestions about how they wish to re-present their favorite book to the class, or to a larger group — say a group of 8, 12 or 16. What is important at this stage is that the re-presenting in verbal, visual or dramatic modes is seen by the students as a critical art. It is critical in that students must make decisions about the mode (mixed or multi-modes) chosen to represent one character, one moment, the whole story or one stage in it.

Other individual response activities could follow. For example, the students could be asked to select one book they would like to buy as a present for one member of their family. Then they could be asked to write an account of both the person and the book, and to give reasons for connecting that person with that book.

Another critical response activity is to ask each group to apply Aiden Chambers' framework of likes, dislikes, patterns and puzzles. They could work through the framework by listing their responses under each of those headings. When the four lists are complete, they could make connections or webs linking ideas or concepts across the columns. Such a procedure could be used as a pre-writing activity. Because the procedure enables students to explore their own personal responses and to share their private insights, they will now be in a better frame of mind to write a more sophisticated or informed response. The salient features of such an experience for the whole class are, first, the provision of a rich book-sharing experience and, second, the provision of a context to extend and explore the pleasure of the text by generating a sea of book talk.

POPULAR PICTURE BOOKS

Listed here are works that have proved popular in secondary schools. No list is ever complete, but this one may serve to introduce the main authors, illustrators and publishers.

Sue Alexander, *Nadia the Willful* (Pantheon Books).
Aliki, *How a Book is Made* (HarperCollins).
Joy Anderson, *Juma and the Magic Jinn* (Lothrop, Lee & Shepard).
Jan Andrews, *Very Last First Time* (Macmillan).
Molly Bang, *Dawn* (Wm. Morrow & Co.).
Molly Bang, *The Paper Crane* (Greenwillow).
Raymond Briggs, *Gentleman Jim* (Hamish Hamilton).
Raymond Briggs, *The Tin Pot General and The Iron Woman* (Hamish Hamilton).
Raymond Briggs, *When the Wind Blows* (Penguin).
Anthony Browne, *Gorilla* (Alfred A. Knopf).
Anthony Browne, *Willy the Wimp* (Alfred A. Knopf).
Gelett Burgess, *The Little Father* (Farrar, Straus & Giroux).
F.H. Burnett (adapted by J. Howe), *The Secret Garden* (Random House).
Barbara Cooney, *Chanticleer and the Fox* (Thomas Crowell).
Susan Cooper, *The Selkie Girl* (Macmillan).
Marcus Crouch, *The Whole World Storybook* (Oxford University Press).
Roald Dahl, *Revolting Rhymes* (Bantam).
Tomie de Paola, *The Clown of God* (Harcourt Brace Jovanovich).
Helen Exley, *What It's Like To Be Me (Disabled Children)* (Friendship Press).
Joan Finnigan, *Look! The Land is Growing Giants* (Tundra Books).
Paul Fleischman, *The Birthday Tree* (HarperCollins).
Mirra Ginsburg, *The Magic Stove* (Putnam).
Margaret Greaves, *Once There Were No Pandas — A Chinese Legend* (Metheun).

Virginia Hamilton, *The People Could Fly — American Black Folktales* (Alfred A. Knopf).

Florence Parry Heide, *The Problem with Pulcifer* (HarperCollins).

Florence Parry Heide, *The Shrinking of Treehorn* (Dell).

W.H. Hooks, *Moss Gown* (Houghton Mifflin).

Ted Hughes, *What is the Truth?* (Faber & Faber).

Charles Keeping, *Railway Passage* (Oxford University Press).

Charles Keeping and Kevin Crossley-Holland, *Beowulf* (Oxford University Press).

Dayal Kaur Khalsa, *Tales of a Gambling Grandma* (Tundra Books).

William Kurelek, *They Sought a New World* (Tundra Books).

William Kurelek and Margaret S. Engelhart, *They Sought a New World* (Tundra Books).

Jane Langston, *The Hedgehog Boy — A Latvian Tale* (Harper & Row).

Robert Lawson, *They Were Strong and Good* (Viking).

Jeanne M. Lee, *Toad is the Uncle of Heaven — A Vietnamese Folktale* (Henry Holt & Co.).

Michele Lemieux, *What's That Noise* (Morrow).

Riki Levinson, *Watch the Stars Come Out* (E.P. Dutton).

Mariana Meyer, *The Little Jewel Box* (Dial).

Jorg Muller and Jorg Steiner, *The Sea People* (Victor Gollancz).

Alice and Marrin Provensen, *The Glorious Flight* (Viking).

Alvin Schwartz, *In a Dark, Dark Room and Other Scary Stories* (HarperCollins).

Sally Scott, *The Magic Horse* (Greenwillow).

William Steig, *Amos and Boris* (Puffin).

William Steig, *Dr. DeSoto* (Farrar, Straus, & Giroux).

Tomi Ungerer, *Moon Man* (Delacorte).

Chris Van Allsburg, *The Polar Express* (Houghton Mifflin).

Chris Van Allsburg, *The Wreck of the Zephyr* (Houghton Mifflin).

Chris Van Allsburg, *The Mysteries of Harry Burdock* (Houghton Mifflin).

Bernard Waber, *Mice on My Mind* (Houghton Mifflin).

Jill Paton Walsh, *Lost and Found* (Andre Deutsch).

Tim Wynne-Jones, *Zoom Away* (Douglas & McIntyre).

Tim Wynne-Jones, *Zoom at Sea* (Douglas & McIntyre).

Jane Yolen, *Sleeping Ugly* (Putnam).

Jane Yolen, *The Girl who Loved the Wind* (HarperCollins).

Jane Yolen, *The Seeing Stick* (HarperCollins).

Margot Zemach, *Jake and Honeybunch Go to Heaven* (Farrar, Straus & Giroux).

Shakespeare: A Multi-Modal Experience

The resources for teaching Shakespeare's plays have never been so rich and diversified. School English departments, as well as individual teachers, have the responsibility to conduct an active search for and build up a pool of these resources. Budget and time constraints are important factors here. Wise, informed selection of teaching resources is critical. Team involvement in the selection of the plays themselves and in the co-ordination and sequencing of them at successive grade levels, and at different levels of instruction, is perhaps the first step in planning and providing an optimum experience for our students. Of course, there is no master plan by which the various plays are allocated to particular grades. Individual teacher interest and enthusiasm will be a guiding factor.

Once a department has reached consensus on the allocation of the plays, the next step might be to choose the particular editions of the plays to be provided. Every English department has had various experiences using the editions available. The personal preferences of teachers will again play a key role. Replacement of worn-out series or class sets provides an opportunity for wise choice.

Among the more widely recognized and adopted editions are:

- *The HBJ Shakespeare Series.* Series Editor: Ken Roy (Harcourt Brace Jovanovich, Canada).
- *The Oxford School Shakespeare.* Series Editor: Roma Gill (Oxford University Press, England).

Perhaps a more difficult task is the selection of the audio-visual resources to be used. For each play to be taught, it is desirable to have:

- a visual presentation of the entire play on video cassette or film;
- a vocal presentation of the entire play on audio tape cassette, compact disc or records;
- a reliable school edition of the play to provide a verbal presentation of the play.

Only through multi-modal experiences of the text can a student come to a fuller enjoyment and appreciation of Shakespeare. Verbal text, vocal (or spoken) text, and visual or fully enacted text — complete with sets, costumes, staging, props, lighting, casting and directing — should all be made available. Teachers need to be not only discerning in the planning and provision of these experiences, but also cognizant of the differences in experience of the play that each modality provides.

Teachers develop their own preferences in selecting and planning a sequence of activities, but it normally follows the stages outlined below.

Initial Experience: Visual Presentation

This may be arranged so that all students taking the same play see the same film together. If a video can be used, however, the problems of arranging a large block of time for a large group may be circumvented. Nevertheless, it is still desirable to provide a period of time long enough for students to experience the play from beginning to end without interruption.

Vocal Presentation Of the Play

This may be segmented into units that fit into the regular timetable. Teachers should plan the segments carefully so that this phase does not drag on interminably. Longer, sustained stretches are preferable to short scenes interrupted by textual questions and discussion.

Readers' Theatre

Working in groups, or pairs, students should choose a portion of the play that they will rehearse in their own time for presentation to the class.

Exploring the Text

With some classes, teachers may wish to invite the students into a deeper exploration of Shakespeare's language. Similarly, there may be passages in the play that the teacher wishes to investigate more closely. Perhaps the teacher may want to reinforce what it is that the playwright-poet can *do, say* and *mean* with language. For instance, how does a character say one thing but clearly intend another? How can a line or passage hint at diverse, divergent or even contradictory meanings? How does the form, pattern or structure of the text fit, reinforce or even reverse the speaker's intention? What technical terms, concepts or tools will students need in order to appreciate more fully the craft of the text?

71

The practical answers to these questions depend upon the teacher's judgment and literary experience. However, if teachers apply the small group investigative strategies recommended for poetry (see specifically Patrick Dias, page 50; Doug Hilker, page 52; and Ryder Payne, page 53) they will create a classroom context in which will emerge those teachable moments — those moments where it is just right for the teacher to intervene and show a technical term, concept or device that students do not already have.

These teachable moments occur as the teacher listens in on small group discussions or presentations. With sensitive conferencing and mini-lessons, teachers can follow the lead their students provide in order to guide them in technical matters.

6. Working with Reluctant Readers

Typical Kinds of Reluctance

In almost every classroom, there are students who are reluctant or impeded readers. It is worth looking at the most common types of reluctance before considering the most effective strategies for dealing with those reading problems.

Readers with Negative Attitudes

Most teachers have encountered students who don't read or won't read. These are students who in spite of all previous schooling — and in some cases, because of it — do not have the reading habit. As yet, they have not discovered the joys of reading nor have they any desire to do so. Although they come to school each day, reading finds little or no place in their daily lives. The challenge for the teacher is to provide a reading experience that will offer satisfaction and a sense of achievement.

Word Callers

Some students, when asked to read for the teacher during a reading conference, seem to demonstrate some proficiency until they are asked to explain the passage in their own words. With or without the book, they are unable to retell. This type of reader is often baffling to the teacher. During the oral reading these students sound reasonably confident, but they have little idea what the passage is all about. These are the word callers. They have responded to those unhelpful lessons which directed them to get every word right rather than helping them to make sense of the text. No wonder reading is such a dissatisfying experience for them. They are in urgent need of sustained one-on-one help. The teacher does not always have time for sustained conferencing and demonstrations. For both the teacher and student, the best provision is often peer tutoring (see page 81).

Text Plodders

Some students really "mess up" during the oral reading. Miscues or errors abound in every sentence. These students are painfully aware of most of their mistakes and attempt some self-correction. However, their self-image as readers is seriously diminished as they slavishly try to get everything right. Generally the teacher intervenes after a few anxious moments to acknowledge that this is a poor choice of text. It is much too difficult — frustrating even. The student is asked to try again with something much simpler, which he or she can read easily. However, the simpler text does not present the same satisfaction or cognitive challenge, and the reader feels devalued by the compromise. What seems to be kindness, or even compassion, on the part of the teacher may be more of a hinderance than a help to such students. The teacher's patience and persistence until the end of the passage may be the best support for such students, for when invited to retell the story, these students often produce amazing evidence of comprehension.

Non-Readers

There are also students who are virtually non-readers. The best provision a teacher can make for such students in their adolescent years is daily one-on-one book sharing, in which the "secrets of reading" are demonstrated to non-readers and emulated by them. Once again, peer tutoring is an ideal way to provide such individualized attention (see page 81).

All of the types of readers examined here have usually become quite competent in developing masking or coping skills. Many of them do not want to call attention to their problems, or to themselves, and they will get from their friends the notes, the answers or the information they need to keep up appearances. They become skilled at conning their teachers, making excuses and getting by. But, in fact, they are falling through the cracks for want of discerning assessment and treatment.

What follows, then, are strategies to transform these various types of reluctant or impeded readers into a community of learners capable of sustained and productive engagement with literature texts.

The Literature Workshop

So much depends upon the teacher's general attitudes, beliefs and expectations of both students and books. If the teacher expects maximum resistance to books, that is probably what the teacher will get — a minimal or discouraging response to all motivational efforts. But if the teacher truly believes in the power of books, the power of stories to transform the most hardened and loathing student, then the collective response will be truly amazing. This is the experience of teachers such as Liz Waterland (1985) in England and Nancy Atwell (1987) and Cora Five (1986) in the United States. These teachers trusted in the power of books. They also trusted in their students to become "hooked on books" once they became aware of the pleasures they offered.

Fundamental to the thinking of these teachers is the realization that if teachers provide the condition of learning, students will learn. If we provide the conditions of reading and writing, they will read and write. If we provide the tools and techniques for literary development, every student will develop the ability to use them.

Setting up the Literature Workshop

The first step in setting up the literature workshop is to provide a classroom collection of good books and great reads for young people. How many books? A good rule of thumb is about five titles per student, so in a classroom of 30, there should be a minimum of about 150 books. This collection is not a static one by any means. New books are constantly added as they become available, whether bought from book stores and publishers or borrowed from the school library. What kind of books? This matter is as important as the number of books, so teachers should keep the following criteria in mind as they build up the collection.

1. Multi-level books. The reading abilities of any given class will range from several years below grade level to several years

above, so the books provided should match the multi-level range of abilities with a similar range of readability.
2. Multi-genre books. In any given class, the range of reading interests will be more diverse than the range of reading ability, so the kinds of books selected should be as diverse as possible to provide a rich variety of literary experiences. A short list of genres would include the usual kinds of fiction now popular with young people: adventure, romance, mystery, horror, humour, fantasy, science fiction and utopian literature. In addition to these popular kinds, teachers would be wise to include myths, legends, fairy tales, plays, poetry and short stories. Many myths, folk tales and legends are now appearing in picture-book format. Recently some picture books have been developed for use by older students. They have a powerful appeal to adolescents and can serve to demonstrate some of the more subtle aspects of literary theory. Provisions should also be made for those students who prefer more factual reading, such as information books, historical fiction and biography.
3. Multi-cultural books. The classroom book collection should be chosen to reflect the linguistic and cultural diversity of the students in class as well the diversity of ethnic groups in the school community.

Approaches to the running of successful literature workshops are as varied as the teachers who run them. There is no right way, or one way. However, all teachers should aim for maximum engagement with the books and among students working together. At the outset of the program, or with a particularly diffident class, it is best to allocate time for silent reading. It is important, too, to establish rule-governed routines for borrowing and returning books to the classroom collection and routines for keeping personal reading records.

Once the students are immersed in a good read, the teacher can begin to introduce them to various kinds of response. Initially the best response strategy is the reader's response journal or dialogue journal, whereby students are invited to explore the patterns or puzzles the book presents. Many students begin with a re-telling of the story, or they adopt a style of writing acquired through years of doing book reports. We should keep in mind that, for many of our students, the experience of books provided in the early years of reading goes a long way in conditioning their early efforts. Once the routines of silent reading and response journals are established, however, the teacher can help students to overcome superficial, or even literal-minded, responses. The teacher can invite students to explore their real feelings about the other worlds and other people presented to them in fiction.

The teacher will come to know the needs of each class and of the different groups within the class, and can then decide how best to meet them. Among the techniques that can be used are the following:

1. Reading conferences, in which the teacher dialogues with one student or with a small group of students.
2. Mini-lessons, in which the teacher demonstrates, by using samples of response writing, the advances some students are making in deepening their response.
3. Literature circles, in which students reading the same novel share their views and opinions by talking about the text or by finding in the text support for the views they hold.
4. Listening logs (see page 15), which help to release students from the attempt to find "the right answer." Listening logs allow students to acknowledge that in many human situations there is no single answer, but a range of choices from which to choose. Exploring the options then becomes a rich and engaged process.

As the students feel they have some ownership and control over the books they read and how they may authentically respond to them, there is growing evidence that the classroom has become a community of learners, and that an adequate quantity and developing quality of language is being produced by writing and consumed by reading.

The 50-50 Program

This idea is really quite simple. At the beginning of the year, the teacher simply announces to the class (or to herself) that every student will be expected, over the course of the year, to read 50 books and compose 50 pieces of writing related to the books he or she has read. The choice of the books to be read will be the student's, so long as they meet with the teacher's approval, and the pieces of writing will develop some aspect of the books the students wish to relate to. The pieces of writing will not be book reports, but they will relate to concerns or personal insights that emerge from the books read.

Some teachers may think that this is an unrealistic goal, especially for students who are having reading problems, yet these are the very students who stand to gain most from such a program.

It is important to consider that students have a way of meeting teacher expectations, of knowing or finding out "what counts" with their new teacher. If teacher expectations are fuzzy or minimal, then course outcomes and student achievements will be equally unclear or modest. If little is expected, little will be done; but if more is required, students *will* rise to meet expectations — even if not so readily at first.

We know that there is always a percentage of students — about 30 percent, more or less — who do not read and write adequately for their grade level. There may be a variety of reasons for this failure, but much of the research in this area points to a neglect of these students. When these students are interviewed, they will often claim that no one ever made them learn. Their development was neglected primarily because they never were required to produce or consume appropriate quantities of written language. Moreover, research into thinking skills has found that cognitive challenge — making demands — is essential for cognitive development. The analogy with literacy development is clear: the schools must accept the responsibility of making demands for the amounts and kinds of reading and writing to be done.

Introducing the 50-50 Program

The idea of establishing a quota, or setting a target number, may be irksome to some. Indeed it may give rise to undesirable repercussions in the minds of some parents or some principals. Therefore, it is not essential to announce a given target number at the outset. Some teachers prefer not to establish a number with the class, but only to raise their own expectations and their own standards, and to prevent minimalist thinking on their part. The positive attitude, in itself, will be transferred to the students.

Central to a quantitative program is the provision of classroom time for reading. Experience has shown that the best way to increase time spent reading at home is to increase time spent reading at school. Once reluctant readers are nudged into a book in the classroom, the book takes over and they will want to read on at home. This nudging requires two main elements: a reading environment supported by rules and routines to prevent interruptions and an inviting display of books. The classroom collection that teachers build up over the years should eventually offer something for everyone. Such a collection gives students ownership and control of their reading by allowing them to choose the books they will read. It should be pointed out that students may choose books from other sources: from the school library, from the public library, from book stores and from those available at home. However, all books coming from sources outside the school must meet with the teacher's approval. The reading done in any classroom is part of the school program and is, therefore, always subject to teacher guidance, supervision and approval.

Once students establish control of their reading, they should be given control, too, of their response. As students immerse themselves in books they are literally "bursting at the themes" in their eagerness to share the pleasure they discover within a given novel, a given author or a given genre. The question facing the teacher is how to guide all the excitement into productive channels. A multiplicity of reading experiences generates a multiplicity of channels of response. Forms of response should not be limited to the teacher's repertoire of activities; however, the teacher should have a pool of suggestions available for those uninitiated in the range of choices. Options include writing a response journal or dialogue journal; responding through visual art in the designing of a book jacket or of a fantasy scene; preparing an excerpt for oral performance or readers' theatre; preparing a collage or a film strip; taping a reading; making a short video; juxtaposing images on the overhead projector to create mood effects for a reading. In short, teachers should encourage students to make creative use of what is normally available in any classroom in order to communicate insight and feeling. Students should be allowed to match their responses with their own talents.

Readers' Theatre

Readers' Theatre is an exciting technique by which students breathe life into the inert words of a given text. The students rehearse and present the text for oral performance before a real audience — other members of the class, other classes in the school or younger children at a junior school.

In some teachers' minds, Readers' Theatre is associated with choral reading. For other teachers, it is associated with scripted drama. Because it is a scripted reading or rehearsed oral presentation, Readers' Theatre does bear some resemblance to both choral reading and scripted drama, but it can easily divest itself of the less desirable features and problems of those forms. Unlike choral reading, it is not a teacher-directed performance; unlike scripted drama, it is unencumbered by conventional sets, costumes and staging. It is a more spontaneous, student-selected, student-directed form of reading aloud that provides a different experience of the text to the audience and to the performers.

Readers' Theatre readily lends itself to a diverse range of texts: poems, folk tales, short stories, excerpts from a novel or a play. It can easily be performed by groups of varying sizes: solo, duet, trio, quartet and so forth. Its primary purpose is to explore the prosody and the non-verbal aspects of text by experimenting with how they should be presented. The rehearsed and polished oral presentation of a text is in itself an act of interpretation as well as an act of criticism. It invites the students to make planned choices for the use of facial expressions, gestures, postures and body language, as well as pitch, tone, tenor and loudness.

Introducing Readers' Theatre

A good place to start is with short chants or poems with a strong rhythm or beat. The teacher begins by selecting suitable chants for the class and by placing copies of these in a hat or in a box. One member from each group of students comes to pick out one chant at random. The groups are then given time and space to read the chant over again and again, until they begin to feel the beat and potential variations in how it should be voiced or performed.

The students, quite spontaneously, decide how the reading will be done: in unison, in parts assigned to each, in two groups (or more) alternating back and forth, with repetition — perhaps — of lines and parts. In general, the students manage to do their own coaching, revising of decisions and exploring other suggestions that emerge from the rehearsal. They begin to feel good about what they are creating and become confident in being able to present a pleasing performance. Because chants have a strong beat and often present a sense of play, students easily memorize the text and concentrate on playful accompaniments to the delivery, such as hand clapping, finger-snapping and foot stomping. When the groups return to class, they take turns in presenting their rehearsed performances. Altogether it is a most delightful experience for everyone.

After such an introduction, the students can move on to more ambitious selections from short stories, novels, picture books, folk tales and longer poems. In general, students are capable of making their own selections from novels or short stories. They can decide, as well, which character parts are assigned to whom and how the narration — the parts of the text not in spoken dialogue — will be given. They may decide on a single voice, for example, or a group of voices in unison. In some classes, teachers provide the groups with an audio tape recorder or a camcorder. Students then have the option of preparing a live or a taped performance. They may use the recorder simply to evaluate their own rehearsals before a live presentation.

Peer Tutoring

For those students in our intermediate or senior grades who, for a variety of causes, are still virtually non-readers, swift intervention is essential. It is likely that such students have a record of related problems: irregular attendance, misbehavior, lack of co-operation, and general failure. It is likely that they have been withdrawn to remedial classes or special education programs. Very often in these special programs they have been given reading drills and exercises, but very little real reading. These unhelpful lessons have been part of the problem contributing to the confusion: confusion on the part of the student trying to sort out mixed messages about what reading is, and confusion on the part of the teacher who may still cherish detrimental beliefs about how reading and writing are learned.

There is general agreement on the part of the experts in this area on the following points:

1. There is no "quick fix" or remedy for reading problems.
2. The longer the problem persists, the more difficult it is to treat.
3. Students with reading difficulties, learning disabilities and special needs will learn to read and write *not* by the diagnosis and "treatment" of a deficiency but by the provision of daily one-

on-one book-sharing which provides them with the essential demonstration of the act of reading.

The practice of providing a reading partner or a reading buddy has enjoyed some popularity in our schools over recent years. However, without preparation, supervision and other requirements to sustain the quality of these sessions, they may soon dwindle to a pointless experience for both. What needs attention from the outset is the seriousness of the problem for the reluctant reader, and the potential for personal growth on the part of the tutor as well as the tutee. In schools where the tutoring program is achieving significant results, much attention is given to both tutees and tutors. For example, the same teacher is assigned to teach those classes in which there are potential tutors in the senior grades and those in which there are students needing one-on-one assistance. The teacher then has an opportunity to know both groups and to provide a sensitive matching of tutor with tutee.

The tutors have to be prepared to undertake their role with responsibility and with tact. They must be given an increased understanding of reading and writing processes, and of developing stages within those processes. They must be instructed in both helping and hindering strategies, in order to maximize the first and avoid the latter. In addition, they must be given the tools and techniques that teachers presently use to advantage in the junior grades.

Introducing Peer Tutoring

How can a student tutor share the secrets of reading? At first, ask the tutor to read all of the story to the tutee, because the tutee likely cannot read any of it. At this stage, the tutee should listen and observe what the tutor is doing. The tutor may want to finger-scan the text or to point to key words or recurring words. The tutee will begin to feel how reading sounds, to hear the rhythm of the text, and to notice the pauses between sentences. Once a text becomes more familiar, the tutor may pause before a repeated word in order to prompt the tutee to say it, or to make a guess. As key words, or patterns of words, become more familiar with repetition, the tutor can expect the tutee to chime in while pointing to each word. The tutee should eventually follow the print, get to know some words, turn the pages, say some parts of the story or the rhyme and, finally, recognize exact words.

An outline of the tutor's steps follows.

1. Always approach tutees with the confident expectation that they can learn to read and write. After all, they understand spoken language and they probably already know some things about how written language works and how it is used in everyday signs and situations. Think of the tutee as a co-reader, and invite him or her to behave like a reader.

2. Select books that will provide an enjoyable experience for both of you. The books you choose at first may be picture books, big books, pattern books or story books. These books may be found in your public library, your school library or in the tutee's classroom. Teachers and librarians can help you in making good selections. In any case, you will want to bring along several books and allow the tutee to make a choice.

3. The third step in your role is called book sharing. Find a comfy place to sit together, and make sure that the book is placed so either person can turn the pages easily. You begin by reading the title and author on the cover, by opening the book to the beginning and by starting to read. As you read, you are demonstrating how the print sounds, where the print is found on the page, how layout and direction works and when pages are turned.

4. As you read, you should have some sense that the tutee is observing what you are doing, and is listening to where the story is going, how the text relates to the pictures, and that it is all making sense. You will know all is going well by the interest in the story, by the attentiveness to what you are doing and by a general sense of concentration.

5. You may read all of the story by yourself or you may prompt the tutee to join in, especially when you come to repeated parts, or to repeated words or predictable ones.

6. When you come to the end of the story, always invite tutees to tell you all about it in their own words. Just say, "Tell me all about the story in your own words." Then listen carefully and wait patiently for the tutee to tell you more. You may help the tutee to retell by using such prompts as, "What happened next?", "What else happened?", "Who else was in the story?"

7. Observe the retelling carefully for it is a critical step for both you and the tutee. For the tutee, it is a satisfactory experience: it demands an ability to reconstruct the story. For you as tutor, it is important to discover what level of understanding the tutee is bringing to your shared experience. Remember, retelling is

both an act of understanding and an act of composing. All of us can understand more easily than we can compose.

8. The next step is to let the tutee guide you. Do you simply go on with other stories? Do you go back over some parts of the story you just finished? Do you, together, find key words or repeated words in the text? Do you go back to favorite parts, or funny parts, and read them again? Do you call it quits for the day?

9. After several sessions together, you could invite the tutee to take turns reading back and forth with you. If you come to a tricky part (for the tutee) you take over and read it. There may now be some passages or parts the tutee can read quite well enough alone, even though not every word is right. The tutee may make mistakes or guesses. Be patient. Do not discourage the tutee by correcting every error. Assure the tutee that it is "okay to mess up," and remind him or her that the important thing is to "get the hang of it." The tutee should try to get the overall meaning of what you are reading together. You may be in this stage for some time, but both of you will have a sense of progress.

10. Whatever decisions you make now, always be careful to avoid anything which could give a sense of failure or discouragement. Your affirmation of progress is most important to the tutee's success.

Signs of Progress

How will the tutor know that the tutee is learning? Listed below are some of the signs to look for at each successive stage. This list should be used simply as a guide to typical behaviors. Each person develops at his or her own rate and in a unique sequence.

Some Signs of Early Progress

The tutor can be sure of progress in the initial session if the tutee:

- enjoys the book-sharing session;
- listens attentively while being read to;
- observes what the tutor is doing;
- is usually co-operative and friendly;
- offers some comments on pictures or story;
- wants to be read to;

84

- handles a book properly — right side up, turns pages, locates print on page;
- follows tutor's voice or finger pointing;
- recognizes some initial letters or even some words;
- relates the story to own experiences;
- enjoys illustrations or mulls over some details;
- retells some of the story in own words.

Some Signs of Developing Progress

The tutor will aim to help the tutee to:

- select a book for sharing, or bring a book to the session;
- be willing to hold the book and turn pages;
- begin to track words with fingers or eyes;
- notice that some words are the same;
- pick out some words or letters when asked;
- retell the story using some pictures as prompts;
- retell the story with greater detail or thoroughness;
- relate the story to other stories, or to personal experiences;
- talk about the story in some detail;
- respond to patterns in language: repetitions, rhythms or rhymes.

Some Signs of Further Progress and Confidence

The tutor can be sure of further progress in follow-up sessions if the tutee:

- demonstrates a positive attitude to book-sharing sessions;
- is eager to join in echo reading or chiming in on familiar parts;
- self-selects books to be shared;
- brings along other school books for sharing;
- re-reads favorite books or stories;
- makes increasing use of predicting ability;
- responds to a variety of cues in both picture and text;
- uses initial letter cues and word endings;
- uses sight vocabulary;
- takes longer turns reading;
- retells the story with greater accuracy and completeness;
- likes to discuss the story and its details.

Some Signs of Independence

Independence in reading is the goal. So the tutor may well celebrate when the tutee:

- self-selects from a variety of books;
- is willing and able to start the reading;
- tackles larger stretches of text;
- begins to acquire some speed and fluency;
- relies less on finger-pointing or laboring over details;
- skips unknown words, or reads ahead, or goes back for another guess;
- is willing to browse through a book alone;
- can read some parts silently for enjoyment;
- knows parts of a book, chapter, titles, headings, contents table or index;
- knows how to use contents table or index to locate information.

Keeping an Observation Log

Tutors should be asked to keep an observation log. This is the most valid form of positive assessment of the tutee's progress. In the daily or weekly log, tutors record their observations of the tutee's attitudes towards them and towards the book-sharing demonstrations they provide. In addition to attitudes and feelings, tutors should record signs of progress.

The observation log is an essential part of the support tutors provide. Each tutor should have a special notebook for this purpose, and every entry should be dated. The best time to make entries in the observation log is at the end of each book-sharing session. Keeping the log should become an established routine so that the information it contains is as accurate and as comprehensive as it can be. As tutors gain some experience in keeping an observation record, they will become better in selecting and recording the observations that are really telling. They tell about the tutee, they tell about the tutor and they tell about the progress being made by both.

7. A Collegial Note on Collaboration

The English Department as a Community of Readers and Writers

One common feature of school organization that impedes curriculum development is an infrastructure that has been inherited from yesteryear. For example, it is difficult to expect teachers to promote concepts of collaboration and community in the classroom if they are part of a school organization founded on and operated by a top-down or pyramid-based administration. If the staff is not itself organized on a collegial basis wherein each teacher is affirmed as a valuable contributor to the co-operative running of the school, it may be unreasonable to expect teachers to "do unto others" what is not done to them.

  If the school principal does run a tight ship by dictatorial control, it will be all the more crucial for the English department head or chairperson to ensure that this authoritative style is not characteristic of their relationship with colleagues assigned to teach English. We cannot expect teachers to teach for empowerment purposes if they, themselves, do not have greater influence over the decisions that affect them. Therefore, it is a major responsibility of the department head or chairperson to provide a style of leadership that transforms a group of individual teachers into a reading-writing, teaching-learning community. It is essential that the day-to-day interaction of the English staff is founded on principles of trust, friendliness, mutuality, sharing and support. Most especially, the English department head or chairperson should be a wide reader and writer. Within the usual constraints of time, budget and personal energy, he or she should adopt measures and strategies to involve each member of the team in curriculum implementation and professional development activities. The English department office should be a place where teachers meet to read, write, discuss, share and solve mutual problems and concerns.

> Through the reading process there is a continual interplay between modified expectations and transformed memory.
>
> Wolfgang Iser

> Our response to a text is a dynamic process of self-correction: we formulate interpretations we have to modify continually because textual information comes gradually and we have to start inferring, connecting and synthesizing details from the beginning.
>
> Jack Thomson

In order to teach students how to become better readers and writers of literature, teachers need to practice, demonstrate and comment explicitly on how they read and write themselves. This requires an ability to articulate the theories that guide their practice as well as a capacity to make these theories available to their students and colleagues too. Therefore, the engagement of teachers together in investigating the literary act and response is essential to the personal development of all English educators.

In some schools this process has somehow been implanted and is thriving. Teachers share their understanding and support each other in new undertakings. Some teachers have become acknowledged leaders in particular aspects of the English program, such as co-operative learning in small groups at various levels of instruction. In other schools there seems to be no sense of cohesion, no sense of membership in a teaching/learning community. There are, however, some definite steps a department head or assistant head can take toward building such a community. The field of English has always been broad and diverse. Moreover, the number of new books produced in a year is overwhelming. Add to this the number of scholarly or practical journals and the number of methodological and technological innovations, and the picture becomes truly bewildering. Faced with this situation some heads and assistant heads, in a truly collegial manner, foster the "local expert" strategy. Each teacher chooses by interest or experience one area in which to specialize — to read more intensively, to keep informed and to keep others informed of significant development in that area.

There is no prescribed list of suitable areas of specialization, but some heads would agree on the following inclusions:

- regional literature;
- multicultural literature;
- feminist literature and critical theories;
- young adult fiction;
- science fiction;
- children's books and picture books;
- poetry publications;
- mythologies;
- critical theories;
- linguistic theories;
- literacy and oracy;
- videotapes and films;
- computer applications and software.

The experts in these areas are given time at departmental meetings to share information and present informal reports. In addition, a portion of the budget is allocated to the purchase of major studies and reports, journals, reviews and newsletters. Some examples are listed in the bibliography.

Bibliography

BOOKS

Atwell, Nancie (1987). *In the Middle: Writing, Reading and Learning with Adolescents.* Portsmouth, NH: Heinemann.

Barron, Marlene (1991). *I Learn to Read and Write the Way I Learn to Talk.* New York: Richard C. Owen.

Barton, Bob & David Booth (1990). *Stories in the Classroom.* Markham, Ont.: Pembroke Publishers. Portsmouth, NH: Heinemann.

Benton, Michael & Geoff Fox (1985). *Teaching Literature: Nine to Fourteen.* Oxford: Oxford University Press.

Bruner, Jerome (1986). *Actual Minds, Possible Worlds.* Cambridge, Mass.: Harvard University Press.

———— (1990). *Acts of Meaning.* Cambridge, Mass.: Harvard University Press.

Chambers, Aidan (1984). Introducing Books to Children. London: Heinemann.

———— (1985). *Booktalk.* London: The Bodley Head.

Dias, Patrick X. (1987). *Making Sense of Poetry: Patterns in the Process.* Ottawa: Canadian Council of Teachers of English.

Dias, Patrick & Mike Hayhoe (1988). *Developing Response to Poetry.* Milton Keynes: Open University Press.

Dixon, John & John Brown (1984). *Responses to Literature: What is Being Assessed?* London: Newcombe House, School Curriculum Development Committee.

Duckworth, Eleanor (1987). *"The Having of Wonderful Ideas" and Other Essays on Teaching and Learning.* New York: Teachers College Press.

Fish, Stanley E. (1980). *Is There a Text in This Class?* Cambridge, Mass.: Harvard University Press.

Frye, Northrop (1972). *On Teaching Literature.* New York: Harcourt, Brace.

Grugeon, Elizabeth & Peter Walden (1983). *Literature and Learning.* East Grinstead, Sussex: Ward Lock Educational.

Hayhoe, Mike & S. Parker (1984). *Working With Fiction.* London: Edward Arnold.

Iser, Wolfgang (1978). *The Act of Reading: A Theory of Aesthetic Response.* Baltimore: Johns Hopkins University Press.

Kahn, Elizabeth, C.C. Walter & L. Johannessen. *Writing About Literature.* Urbana: National Council of Teachers of English.

Meek-Spencer, Margaret (1988). *How Texts Teach What Readers Learn.* Stroud: The Thimble Press.

———— (1991). *On Being Literate.* London: The Bodley Head.

Parsons, Les (1990). *Response Journals.* Markham, Ont.: Pembroke Publishers/Portsmouth, NH: Heinemann.

Probst, Robert (1988). *Response and Analysis: Teaching Literature in the Junior and Senior High School.* Portsmouth, NH: Boynton-Cook.

Rogoff, B. (1990). *Apprenticeship in Thinking.* New York: Oxford University Press.

Rosen, Betty (1988). *And None of it Was Nonsense.* London: Scholastic.

Rosen, Harold (1984). *Stories and Meaning.* Sheffield, England: National Association for the Teaching of English.

Rosenblatt, Louise M. (1976). *Literature as Exploration.* Third Edition. New York: Noble and Noble.

———— (1978). *The Reader, The Text, The Poem: Literary Work.* Edwardsville: Southern Illinois University Press.

———— (No date). *Stories and Meanings.* Papers in Education. London: National Association of Teachers of English.

Squire, James R. (ed.) (1968). *Response to Literature.* Dartmouth Seminar Paper. Urbana: National Council of Teachers of English.

Suleiman, S. & I. Cropsman (eds.) (1982). *The Reader in the Text: Essays on Audience and Interpretation.* Princeton: Princeton University Press.

Tchudi, Stephen (1984). *Language, Schooling and Society.* Proceedings of the International Federation for the Teaching of English Seminar, East Lansing, Michigan.

Thomson, Jack (1986). *Understanding Teenagers Reading: Reading Processes and the Teaching of Literature.* Sydney, Australia: Croom Helm.

Waterland, Liz (1985). *Read with Me: An Apprenticeship Approach.* Stroud: The Thimble Press.

Whale D.B. & T.J. Gambell (1985). *From Seed to Harvest: Looking at Literature.* Ottawa: Canadian Council of Teachers of English.

ESSAYS AND ARTICLES

Britton, James (1968). "Response to Literature" in James Squire (ed.), *Response to Literature.* Dartmouth Seminar Paper. Urbana: National Council of Teachers of English.

Bunbury, Rhonda M. (1986). "Always a Dance Going on in the Stone": An Interview with Russell Hoban in *Children's Literature in Education,* Vol. 17, No. 3: 147-148.

Dixon, John (1985). "What Counts as Response?" in D.B. Whale & T.J. Gambell, *From Seed to Harvest: Looking at Literature.* Calgary: Canadian Council of Teachers of English.

Fillion, Bryant (1981). "Reading as Enquiry" in *English Journal,* January 1981: 39-45.

Five, Cora Lee (1986). "Fifth Graders Respond to a Changed Reading Program" in *Harvard Educational Review,* Vol. 56, No. 4:395-405.

Gambell, T.J. (1986). *English Quarterly,* Vol. 19, No. 2. (All essays in this issue are on teaching literature by T.J. Gambell.) Calgary Canadian Council of Teachers of English.

Harker, John (1985). "The New Imperative in Literary Criticism" in *Visible Language,* Vol. 19, No. 3: 356-372.

Langer, J.A. (1990). "The Process of Understanding: Reading For Literary and Informative Purposes" in *Research in the Teaching of English,* No. 24: 229-260.

Lewis, David (1990). "The Constructedness of Texts: Picture Books and the Metafictive" in *Signal: Approaches to Children's Books,* No. 62, May 1990: 131-146.

Meek-Spencer, Margaret (1982). "Children's Literature: Mainstream Text or Optional Extra?" in Robert D. Eagleson (ed.), *English in the Eighties*: 114-127. Adelaide, Australia: Association for the Teaching of English.

Probst, Robert E. (1986). "Mom, Wolfgang and Me: Adolescent Literature, Critical Theory and the English Classroom" in *English Journal,* October 1986: 33-39.

Protheroe, Brenda (No date). "Six Magic Words" in *Growing with Books in the Formative Years and Beyond.* Ontario: Ministry of Education.

Scholes, Robert (1987). "Textuality: Power and Pleasure", in *English Education,* May 1987:73.

Thomson, Jack (1984). "Wolfgang Iser's 'The Act of Reading' and the Teaching of Literature" in *English in Australia,* December 1984: 18-30.

Travers, D.M. (1984). "The Poetry Teacher, Behaviour and Attitudes" in *Research in the Teaching of English,* No. 18: 367-384.

Wells, Gordon (No date). "Stories are for Understanding" in *Growing with Books in the Formative Years and Beyond.* Ontario Ministry of Education.

_____ (1991). Talk for Learning and Teaching. Paper presented at the International Convention on Language and Literacy, University of East Anglia, April 6-10.